THE NEW PAGE

THE NEW PAGE

FEDERICO MAYOR

With the collaboration of Tom Forstenzer
Foreword by Ilya Prigogine

Dartmouth

UNESCO
Publishing

Published jointly by the United Nations
Educational, Scientific and Cultural Organization
7 Place de Fontenoy, 75700 Paris, France

and

Published by
Dartmouth Publishing Company Limited
Gower House
Croft Road
Aldershot
Hants GU11 3HR
England

Dartmouth Publishing Company
Old Post Road
Brookfield
Vermont 05036
USA

British Library Cataloguing in Publication Data
Mayor, Federico
  New Page
  I. Title
  327

Library of Congress Cataloging-in-Publication Data
Mayor, Federico.
        The new page / Federico Mayor ; with the collaboration of Tom R.
    Forstenzer ; foreword by Ilya Prigogine.
            p.   cm.
        Includes index.
        ISBN 1-85521-652-3 (Dartmouth) : $39.95 (approx.). – ISBN
    9231029495 (UNESCO)
        1. Peace. 2. International relations. 3. Cold War.
    I. Forstenzer, Thomas R. II. Title.
    JX1952.M332   1995
    327–dc20   94–38944
                                                                            CIP
UNESCO Publishing ISBN: 92–3–102949–5
Dartmouth Publishing ISBN: 1 85521 652 3

Printed and bound in Great Britain by
Biddles Ltd, Guildford and King's Lynn

Contents

Foreword

It is a great privilege to write a short foreword for *The New Page*. This book is an impassioned plea for a future in which the civilization of war would be replaced by a culture of peace. Traditionally, our world has been divided into independent states pursuing their own interests through all measures, including war. However, in the past such men as Kant and Wilson dreamed of a time when this sad situation would be modified through the action of international organizations. War would then be replaced by negotiations based on mutual understanding.

Federico Mayor emphasizes that history does not move gradually, but in leaps. As is well known in physics, there exist singular points at which a given situation gives rise to multiple possibilities. Such points correspond to bifurcation points and are widely studied in modern physics. No doubt we are today at a transition point. This has many causes, such as the dramatic increase of the population and the changes in our modes of communication. Bifurcation points are known to be the result of instabilities in situations where small effects may determine what is to happen for a long time to come. In the present context, the history of our planet will probably depend on measures taken on the international scene over the next few years. Hence the feeling of urgency which permeates *The New Page*.

It may be interesting to note that we are also turning 'a new page' in science. We are beginning to overcome the traditional views of science which are ultimately based on a pessimistic vision of nature, leading to the well-known split between the 'two cultures' the scientific and the humanistic. The concept of *laws of nature* has played an essential role in the development of Western science. This is a specific feature of Western thought. In the Chinese tradition, nature means 'that which is by itself'. How, then, can one speak of 'laws of nature'? Yet the concept of laws of nature has been shown to be immensely successful, starting with the classical physics associated with Newton's law and continuing into the 20th century with quantum physics and relativity. These traditional formulations are associated with concepts of determinism and time symmetry. Determinism means that, if we could know the present, we could then predict the future, as well as calculate

vii

the past. Time reversibility means that the present and the future play the same role.

However, there is no way to include *becoming* in such a picture of nature. The universe *is*, it does not become. Certainly the picture has great appeal, but there is a high price to pay for it. Creativity and novelty become illusions. The words I am writing at this very moment would have been pre-programmed at the instant of the Big Bang. Reason is identified with certainty and ignorance with probability.

In spite of all the success of Western science, this is a pessimistic view of the universe which leads to Cartesian dualism and, therefore, also to a dualism in human culture. In the 19th century, a different concept of nature was proposed, one based on the famous Second Law of Thermodynamics: the law of the increase of entropy. But what does this 'increase of entropy' mean? In a recent film based on a best-selling book, a simple example is proposed. Suppose we take a cup of tea and throw it on the ground: it breaks. Instead of a single unit, the cup of tea, we have many pieces: this corresponds to the appearance of 'disorder'. The essence of the Second Law would be precisely in that appearance of disorder. Can this be the whole story? It is true that we occasionally break some china, but surely we produce more cups than we break! Is the production of cups, therefore, an anti-entropic event? This would again be a deeply pessimistic view, since the only predictable state of the universe would be the maximum state of disorder, 'heat death'.

Fortunately, we are beginning to overcome these pessimistic views. An important step has been the birth of a new science, the science of complexity. This science describes the remarkable self-organization which occurs in systems far from equilibrium. One of the conclusions of the science of complexity is the importance of the time vector. It shows the constructive role of the 'arrow of time'. Moreover, the science of complexity deals with non-linear situations. There are many solutions to basic equations. As Federico Mayor emphasizes, novelty occurs in leaps. The future is not given. The local fluctuations associated with instability may play an essential role in the subsequent evolution of the system as a whole.

Some 40 years ago, the number of scientists involved in solid state physics and information science may have been in the order of a few hundred. Today, these fields have grown to a level of importance that may have a determining impact on human history. There has been a huge increase in the numbers of specialists involved, greater than any other we have previously experienced, including the spread of Buddhism and Christianity.

As a result of the new insights we have gained from these fields, we must revise our views of the laws of nature. Instead of expressing certitudes, they must now be seen to represent 'possibilities'. This has always been the case within the humanities and social sciences. We cannot predict the future, but we can prepare it. As the great French poet, Paul Valéry, has written: 'the future is construction'. Human action depends on our memory of the past, our analysis of the present and our anticipation of the future. All three aspects are included in *The New Page*.

The New Page is a manifesto preparing us for the next century in a spirit of collaboration among the great cultural traditions of the past. Let us hope that the volume will receive the attention it deserves.

I. PRIGOGINE

To construct peace or democracy,
we are beginning to understand
better and better, is not limited
to signing treaties, demobilizing
armies, authorizing multi-party
competition or altering institutions.
It is further necessary, it is above
all necessary to make changes in
attitudes and in the image each has
of the other, to transform the way in
which we manage inter-personal
conflicts as much as group conflicts.
At the same time, innovations occur
in particular times, in particular
contexts with particular persons.
Their spread beyond these circumstances
then depends on the broader context.
(Pierre Calame, *Mission possible*)

Introduction

The notion of a 'new page' first occurred to me in 1988 as the first agreements on nuclear non-proliferation and on a genuine reduction in tactical and strategic missiles came within reach. Changes in the world, notably rapid transformation in the then Soviet Union, began to indicate that we were coming to the end of the civilization of war that had dominated the lives of all who have lived through the middle decades of this century. And, of course, an organization of society around violence has marked most of human history down to the present.

Thus, in October 1988, an immense power of destruction was, perhaps for the first time in human history, being dismantled precisely because of the enormity of the risk it entailed for our species. This extraordinary momentum, however tentative and fragile, was appearing as we neared the end of a century and, indeed, the beginning of a new millennium. Moreover, the cold war's end went hand-in-hand with an even more fragile birth, or rebirth, of democracy, not only in Europe, but in Asia, Africa and Latin America.

In fact, on the very day that the Berlin wall came tumbling down in late 1989, I sent a UNESCO official to Africa to speak there with five heads of state on my behalf. The message I wished to share was that 'the winds of freedom are blowing now throughout the world and that democracy will clearly be on the African agenda'.

The 'new page' which we are turning in this book is one of a culture of peace, based on a culture of democracy. It is a transition fraught with all the dangers of moving into the unknown without much guidance from our personal or collective memories. If this transition can be successful, we will at long last have the possibility of changing radically our economic, social and political perceptions and entering a new renaissance of hope and creativity in our lifetimes. It would be foolish (and self-limiting) to try to predict precisely the outcome of such a process. As Alejo Carpentier wrote, 'El hombre nunca sabe para quien padece y espera' ('Man never knows for whom he labours and waits'). But it is clear that the beginning of this 'new page' can be written by all of us living right now. A movement away from war to peace also means a transition from societies dominated by the state, sole organizer of security in a dangerous world, to the civil society of everyday life:

where individuals work and create and invent the texture of their lives in their local communities freed from the fears of the 'war culture'.

The state, and the international system of inter-state relations, will slowly give up the stage to the non-governmental, private and voluntary communities. Governments will carry out the watchtower functions of ensuring that certain basic, democratically agreed rules are respected, but more and more the individual and the local community will become more directly involved in decision making. In Hegelian terms, we will move from being 'subjects' to becoming 'actors'.

My work as Director-General of UNESCO has made it necessary for me to work with decision-makers throughout the world. I have discussed world affairs, and particularly education, science, culture and communication, with 110 heads of state or government over the last six years. I have had the opportunity to talk with them at some length, to know them as people facing formidable challenges. I came to admire the strength of conviction and breadth of vision that some of them project. In almost all cases, I shared their sense of loneliness and frustration in grappling with difficult problems within the context of fragile decision-making structures. Even the very best of the world's leaders must often work patiently within governmental bureaucracies that tend to limit the horizon for action to next week, next month or next year.

It is clear to me and, I believe, to many leaders that solutions to our present-day problems will require far more precise, scientific knowledge than is currently available within governments. Moreover, this knowledge must be used to provide a long-term vision of trends and options available to decision makers as opposed to 'getting by' or 'muddling through' the mini-crises of each season or year.

What matters now is less the past than the future. A new renaissance can only be created by perseverance, daring and knowledge. Each has a role to play and each of us must try to combine these qualities as we deal with problems, global and local alike. I often say that 'risk without knowledge is dangerous, but knowledge without risk is useless'. Perhaps the one obsession I have developed and treasured all my life is a horror of a good day lost, time wasted. Too often, our capacity to act is paralysed by an incapacity to feel intensely the suffering in our immediate setting and the massive injustice experienced by the poorest people in the poorest countries. We deny what we know exists, retreat from the challenge of life pulsing all around us and slide comfortably into a kind of paralysis.

It was Antonio Gala who regretted 'the lost good days' and Arthur Rimbaud who summed up such a feeling in retrospect: 'by being too sensitive I have wasted my life'. To struggle against such lassitude, often clothed in the academic or political guise of awaiting perfect knowledge and wasting valuable time for action in report after report (what I call the reporting society), the perseverance and commitment of a rebel is necessary. It requires a fusion between politics and ethics – which is expressed best in a French pun I use, 'pol-éthiques'. Ethics should imbue our political acts with an openness and imagination which summon us to act quickly to confront such major problems of our time as uncontrolled population growth, mass migration within and between countries, environmental degradation and poverty. The solution to these and other problems is becoming more and more evident. It is education for all, and particularly for women and girls.

The qualities that shine through such people who have marked our times as Nelson Mandela, F.W. De Klerk, Mikhail Gorbachev, Shimon Peres, Yasser Arafat, Gro Harlem Brundtland and others are the energy and stubbornness to move towards action when others would continue to hesitate. In my meetings with each of them, and in my own experience, I have learned that history does not move gradually but rather in sudden rapid leaps of events that surprise everyday routine and challenge the imagination. To be prepared for the unexpected, to resist the docility and apparent security of routine remain responsibilities for all who wish to benefit from present circumstances to help spark a renaissance of peace and hope. Perhaps the best image, however tragic, of the errors implicit in blind faith is the sinking of the *Titanic* on the night of 14/15 April 1912. The band bravely played 'Fascination', a ragtime hit of the day, as the mighty ship took them and so many others down to the deep. The technology of the day, including the watertight compartment and the wireless, proved useless to stop the tragedy.

There is an added risk, that of creating heavy technological and bureaucratic structures driven by pure inertia – 'under their own dynamics', one could say – while the planet is confronted by poverty, fanaticism and environmental degradation. Our scientific, technological and industrial mastery could thus become our own worst enemy. Political power, even more our individual influence, appear irrelevant when faced by these 'great machines' in which so many different types of interest converge.

If the history of humanity has been a succession of struggles against nature for survival, today man faces his own work, his own dangers, that go far beyond the risks of the natural system left to itself. To write a new page, we must rededicate ourselves to the ethical force of peace rather than the coercive force of war. We must not lose sight, despite certain aspects of United Nations peace-keeping activities, of the fact that we are striving to create the moral force of the United Nations, not a United Nations of military forces. Only by striving for a new renaissance locally, nationally and internationally, can perceptions and actions determine the shape of things to come.

Without the discipline of striving to bring all the diverse citizens of all the different countries of the world together in all their plurality, the drive for development could lead to a form of decadence. Tolerance after all is a discipline, as is the constant commitment to look to the essence, the priorities, in situations and problems as the basis for common action. President Diouf of Senegal has written that 'the road to modernity is called perseverance'. Each of us has a responsibility to persevere in our dreams and ideals. 'Because I still think and dream, to think and to dream is never in vain,' said the poet Jose Bergamin. Thus we must speak out, each in our own way and in our own setting, and resist being lulled into docility.

I hope the 'new page' really will be written. A few years ago, the West believed it held solutions. The rest of the world believed the West held solutions. The result, however, was that the 'beacon' could only shine in economic terms in a restricted area and for the short term. Out of this came something very positive: we all learned an important lesson, the need to be constantly alert and watchful.

Politics at every level is emphatically not 'the art of the possible'. It should, in fact, be that perseverant rebellion which seeks every day to put ethics into action and turn dreams into reality. In 1966, Robert Kennedy went to South Africa to speak direct to the young men and women of that troubled country. He said, 'it is from numberless diverse acts of courage and belief that human history is shaped. Each time a man stands up for an ideal, or acts to improve the lot of others, or strikes out against injustice, he sends a tiny ripple of hope, and crossing each other from a million different centres of energy and daring, those ripples build a current which can sweep down the mightiest walls of oppression and resistance.' He did not live to see our time, but we have the responsibility to summon such a tide and sweep forward into the future.

FEDERICO MAYOR

1 Culture of War and Culture of Peace

A new page is being turned in human history and, particularly, in the history of our species' relationship with the planet on which we live. We are being reintroduced to 'time' in a rapid, accelerating sequence of political, social, cultural and environmental events which are changing our perceptions of ourselves as communities and individuals and challenging our confidence to manage global trends.

The pace and direction of these changes are altering – in equally important ways – our systems of perceiving both the human and the physical environment around us. As more and more unexpected and significant sets of information come to our attention, Marshall McLuhan's dictum becomes a concrete reality: 'Information overload; system transformation.' But systems do not 'transform' in a unilinear or reflexive way. Many continue to project a safe and 'known' past onto the future. Others plunge into disorientation, pessimism and despair.

Writing from my individual vantage point, as a scientist, educator, and as the person who heads the United Nations Educational, Scientific and Cultural Organization, I would like to think out loud in these pages – to speak out as a private person in public functions. My views are not presented here in any official capacity, but they draw on the unique perspective of seeing the world as a whole every day, a requirement of my job and the result of a professional career that has moved from the local to the regional to the national and, finally, to the international.

My own experience of transition in my life, in that of my country, Catalonia, and of my nation, Spain, leads me to believe that our world may be facing a sudden and unexpected opportunity to move – rapidly – from a 'culture of war' to a 'culture of peace'. All the habits, disciplines, identities and, of course, investments made in an atmosphere of nearly permanent mobilization for conflict are now moving towards change. 'Security' is being redefined as a civil, even a scientific issue, and no longer seen as a matter of warheads and delivery systems.

As 1989 came to a close, our celebration of the bicentenary of the French Revolution turned into a reliving of an era of sudden, rapid advances of freedom and democracy. Peacefully, in most cases, whole national communities simply shrugged off a political and social system that seemed as if it would last for many generations. These totalitarian systems, with their control of information, their institutionalization (indeed celebration) of the need to police and control the details of private and public life and their vast repressive powers simply evaporated when confronted by massive, peaceful outpourings of the longing to live in free, democratic societies. Even when the most brutal and personalized of those regimes (that of Ceaucescu in Romania) turned to violence in a desperate bid to survive, its own army and Party deserted it and rallied to the defence of popular protest.

These movements in Eastern Europe succeeded because the Soviet Union itself had embarked upon a daring programme of reform and democratization. Leaders in the West have committed themselves to a dynamic of nuclear and conventional disarmament which, as dialogue between the blocs continues, holds out a new, unexpected promise for the future. The armed truce we have been living through for 45 years, based on 'mutually assured destruction' is being replaced by a new approach to security built on 'mutually verifiable arms control'.

While governments, East and West, can begin to think about 'peace budgets' and 'peace dividends', new priorities have been coming to the fore with increasing insistence. The parallel growth of democracy in the Third World, particularly in Latin America and Asia, is threatened by a widespread crisis of development in which debt, prices of raw materials and other factors are wiping out the progress towards growth and better living standards made in the 1960s and 1970s. Poverty is increasing in the poorest countries; school systems are underfinanced and cannot educate the new generation; the number of famished children and illiterate young people continues to grow in too many settings. The end of a bipolar world has also meant the rise of inter-ethnic, inter-religious strife in the former Yugoslavia, former Soviet Union and in Somalia. Peace-keeping has come onto the United Nations agenda as never before.

At the same time, the effects of poverty in the south and 'progress' in the north are driving changes in our planet's life-support systems that threaten the survival of all. From the inefficient burning of fossil fuels in the most advanced societies to the daily necessity of cutting and burning wood to cook the meagre meals of those subsisting in the villages and slums of the least developed countries (LDCs), factors are converging that accelerate global change towards a very real point of no return: the greenhouse effect on our air, oceans and climate. The notion of a point of no return has been so effectively used in science fiction that we must work hard to show the public and decision makers its relevance to science *fact*. The dystopian novels of such gifted seers as Asimov and Zelazny, of Fred Hoyle and Stanislaw Lem, were not meant to dull us to the reality of the questions they probed. In fact, Asimov and Hoyle wrote science fiction against the background of lives spent researching and teaching science. All of these thinkers were contemporaries of the domestic and international tensions of the cold war, but their work used scientifically inspired fancy to draw our attention to the environmental and technical challenges developing at more basic levels of our social existence.

Meanwhile, scientists ranging over such disciplines as theoretical physics, epidemiology, meteorology and mathematics were quietly exploding the 'timeless' Newtonian universe and introducing the idea of chaos – instability in natural and human systems. Time, which is so central to the novelist's story-telling, was returned to science, which must now tell a new, more accurate story about the way nature really works. In an unstable, not entirely predictable natural universe, events do not move at the steady 'tick-tock' of the metronome or mechanical clock. A test-tube reaction, or an earthquake, move at varying pace, slowly building up to a sudden acceleration to the outcome. We may not yet know the early, gathering signs of the oncoming dramatic event, but scientists can indicate the moment at which the reaction – the disaster – becomes irreversible. This point of no return for Earth's climate and life-support systems may be fast approaching.

From the richest countries, with enormous scientific and technical know-how and resources, to the poorest, lacking for the most part in the most basic human skills and infrastructures, the environmental moment of irreversibility will announce a shared catastrophe. All will be relatively equal before the implacable force of rising seas and chronic drought – outcomes of a climate heated beyond the natural level which nurtures the human species. This global change will have been largely the result of human interaction with the atmosphere, the water and the soil that, for millennia, gave us life. This thin and fragile biosphere formed the basis for the many different forms of social organization, production, value systems and religious belief s we call 'cultures'. Our accelerating demographic growth, our needs for fuel and food and shelter are driving the process more and more rapidly to a point of no return.

We must act quickly and comprehensively to prevent the dynamic of irreversibility from taking hold. Finite and diminishing 'world enough and time' remain for us to affirm life and to meet our intergenerational responsibilities to the very young. If not, today' s children and their children may suffer predictable – and preventable – environmental deterioration in the next century. To pull back from the brink, to reverse the build-up of carbon dioxide and other pollutants in our environment, no single nation, however strong, no single institution or set of institutions can succeed alone. Parliaments and political leaders, the mass media and the scientists and technologists will have to transcend the limits of their special callings and work together.

The frontiers between nations mean nothing to the molecules acting on our air and water. Within each political unit, the dividing lines between politics, communications, science and education form unnecessary obstacles to a holistic understanding of a multidimensional problem. Global change means that our highly specialized professions and institutions will have to find common ground in understanding the interconnections between the scientific, social, political and economic facets of the way human behaviour is changing our environment. Only then can efficient solutions be generated and applied.

UNESCO's Constitution, which calls for 'building the defenses of peace in the minds of men', may seem dated against a contemporary history which moved, almost non-stop, from the physical horror of the Second World War to the permanent threat of nuclear conflict. Somehow, in the brief transition from hot war to cold war, religious and ethical traditions of respect for life and of the community, through education, science, culture and communication, managed to come together in an institution of the United Nations system. Witnesses to the anti-humanism of various forms of Fascism and Nazism, UNESCO's founders believed that knowledge has an ethical foundation and an ethical role to play in building a peaceful world through intellectual cooperation. The perversion of education, science, culture and communication in the celebration of violence and hate – in their mobilization in the most extreme forms of the culture of war – led the framers of UNESCO's Constitution to rededicate learning and creativity to building global communities of tolerance, cooperation and mutual understanding. The renascent culture of war that developed during the cold war did not make UNESCO's vision easy to maintain in a world in which knowledge was increasingly dedicated to fabricating weapons systems of enormous destructive power and sophistication. The division of the world into heavily armed blocs did not facilitate intellectual dialogue.

History is constantly changing direction and pace. This historical flux has opened up vistas and provided us with opportunities that other generations have been denied. We are, simultaneously, the products of a war culture and the potential avatars of a peace culture. In us, in our culture and society, are a set of attitudes and outlooks we must understand, confront and overcome. Humans are not violent by nature. In 1986, I participated in a meeting of scientists in Seville. The Seville Statement concluded, categorically, that there is no scientific evidence whatever that humans are violent because of anything inherent in the organism. Our genes are not to blame. We, as the thinking, feeling, creating animal of the planet, have only ourselves to blame, or to accept and change.

Culture, the symbols, values and messages that are our greatest creation, exists within us more vibrantly than any stone monument. It is a sea of memories, significations and fantasies for the future in which we swim all our lives. And every woman, child and man bathes in it and has the potential, unlike the fish or the dolphin, to change that sea by creating new insights, new ways of seeing, doing and being. The fantastic potential of each human being is that, unlike Ved Mehta's 'Fly in the Fly Bottle', we know we are surrounded by boundaries of our own contrivance and that, therefore, we can escape across them and even smash them forever!

But first, we must see them clearly and understand how they work around us and within us. Our own century is particularly instructive on the war culture. It was born in enormous hope for peace and progress. The end of the 19th century and the first years of the 20th (the last *fin de siècle*) were marked by the most basic and lasting discoveries of our time: the nature of matter, nuclear energy and relativity and the nature of the psyche, our internal dynamics and the irrational. Art, like science and psychiatry, was also breaking out of Victorian constraints and exploring expressionism and abstraction. In political life, democracy and liberalism were making progress in Europe and the first signs of trends towards national independence in the colonial empires were becoming visible.

Our nostalgia for this simpler, more hopeful time is only understandable when we consider what befell it and us. Within it, inside its confident and graceful outer facade, political ambitions, ignorance, fear of the poor and of democratic change and blind patriotism were waiting to sweep reason away. In 1914, the European world of light, science and hope gave way to one of darkness, hatred and destruction. Modern science and industry converged with military aims and ambitions to foster a war of unexpected, seemingly uncontrollable destructive power and duration. Paul Fussell, the Anglo-American scholar, has written about *The Great War and Modern Consciousness*. He argues that it had a greater impact on our ways of thinking than anything, including the nuclear age, that came after.

The industrialization of war into a monstrous, mass enterprise was unexpected. On both the Western and the Eastern fronts, the antagonists confidently predicted wars of movement, bright slashing sorties of plumed hussars and battle lines of colourful infantry. Barbed wire, high explosives, smokeless powder, machine guns and the repeating rifle turned this 19th-century vision of acceptable gallantry into the reality of trenches and stalemated armies seeking camouflage in the colours of mud and smoke. More searing to contemporaries and troublesome to our later consciousness, these masses of young men, officered by the most educated generation of middle-class Europeans in history, stepped off, again and again into no man's land to certain destruction.

Victory was measured in metres and casualties in the hundreds of thousands per month.

Science and technology were mobilized to break the stalemate – poison gases, aeroplanes, submarines and the tank. The level of violence and suffering increased and was sustained until the weakest and most backward belligerent societies simply cracked. First Russia, then Austria–Hungary and finally Germany ceased to be imperial monarchies. Even the French army mutinied in 1917. The visions of Blasco Ibanez's *The Four Horsemen of the Apocalypse* and of Erich Maria Remarque's *All Quiet on the Western Front* still haunt our century. Out of collapse came the Bolshevik Revolution, the rise of Fascist movements in Germany, Italy and the successor states of Central Europe and of domestic political extremisms among the liberal democratic 'victors'.

The extremisms of the 1920s and 1930s exalted the state, traded individual dignity for different forms of 'escape from freedom' and rushed headlong towards a Second World War. Armies moved at great speeds to avoid stalemate but ideology and pragmatism joined to widen the war zone to include bombing civilian populations. The first experiments in air attacks on cities and towns took place in my own country. The cold war has taught us to live on ground-zero, with every expectation that the next world war would be the last, ending not in a victory or a peace, but in the silence of the Earth. Yet the cold war stalemate also contributed to the independence of countries that had, until the Second World War, been colonies of European powers. The international scenario, beginning in the early 1960s, became vastly more complex, with new, developing countries opting for alignment with East or West or for non-alignment. Whatever the frequently changing choices, they largely remained technologically dependent on the industrialized countries. And, of course, cold war became hot in all too many Third-World settings.

All this, of course, is history, but while our concern is now and tomorrow, we must carefully examine and even catalogue the baggage we carry out of the past. In our minds, and our hearts, we carry burdens we must discard and limits we must transcend if the future is truly to be different. In a culture of war, all bodies, all mentalities, all souls, if you will, are permanently tensed for the worst. The 'other' in another camp, another country, another continent, is a threat. Differences between individuals and communities become rallying points for mobilization and hatred, not simply the rich pluralism history has given us.

Science, technology, art and communication become weapons or buttresses to secure us from our enemies, and soothe us in the righteousness or superiority of our 'cause' or identity. Government itself, in the state of war or the state of permanent mobilization, is expected to attend to business and protect us with ever more destructive and sophisticated weapons systems. We are told that we can sleep well each night because soldiers, sailors and airmen are awake and ready to launch missiles that ensure that 'they' – the others – will never launch theirs. And even the smallest exchange of warheads, through accident or strategy, could plunge the Earth into nuclear winter. The weapons become so secret that the civilian, non-scientific leadership of nations may not be trusted to understand their own arsenals. Security becomes an obsession – and it is defined as secrecy, unaccountability and dissembling. In the words of Pogo, 'We have met the enemy and he is us!'

Indeed, the culture of war is such that it has pervaded our behaviour in ways other than we might have expected. The culture of war may have taught us certain survival skills in an extremely hostile world, but it may have taught us skills which are poorly adapted to a world which offers new possibilities for our personal achievements, societal progress and world development. One is reminded of the biography of the great Max Weber, to whom we owe recognition as the founder of modern sociology as a discipline. Weber, universally admired for his scholarly abilities, beloved of scholars of comparative religion, historians, philosophers and students, was none the less happiest when, in his day, he could put on his military reservist's uniform and seem to be an ordinary member of what we can only describe as the culture of war. Weber was and is symbolic of an intellect and personality divided between innovation and conformity. This most tolerant of thinkers felt it necessary to appear to be 'an officer and a gentleman' in order fully to enjoy a civic identity. That he was among the foremost thinkers of his time was not enough for him or his milieu.

We too are divided. We have created chasms between people of different skin colours, different ideological persuasions, different religious convictions and different languages. We have adopted ways of producing things and doing business which glorify not the productive aspects of our work but the competitive ones. Competition is useful, competition is even playful, but when raised to the level of seeking the humiliation or the suffering of others, competition is not a proper way in which to pursue the development of a humane world. Perhaps the worst aspect of the culture or war, which even exists in times of peace, is our constant definition of 'us' against 'them', our constant notion that there is a barrier between who we think we are, the people with whom we interact normally and outsiders. Thus we divide the world between hostile groupings in which we tend to identify the outsider (or difference) as something which must be rejected, looked down upon or viewed as a potential threat to our own behaviour.

Indeed, the market with its competitive drives which can often be very useful for innovation and in deciding whether we are efficient or not can also be seen against a military metaphor and therefore denatured into something which is not a test of ourselves against ourselves but rather a test of ourselves against some others. Thus the culture of war, because of its dominance, can also influence our behaviour in peace. It can make us feel in conflict when in fact we should be in playful or constructive competition, not in a life-and-death struggle against outside forces which are somehow made into a threat to our egos or ourselves.

We have attached so many labels onto others – and they onto us – that we may have lost sight of that most basic, enormous truth: the other is a woman, a child, a man, capable of love, uniquely capable of receiving and giving love, uniquely valid and valuable and human. Dare we reach out and take the risk that every major religion and philosophy says we must, the risk of loving and being loved? To retreat or hate is to love death, to reach out and tenderly accept the 'great chain of being' is to affirm life.

For in the midst of this culture of war there were visionaries and rebels who could not or would not conform. They were individuals, men and women, who could understand that war was not necessarily a solution to the problems that confronted their society and their nations. They did not merely abhor war morally, they also understood historically that war has rarely provided a definitive or stable solution to problems between or within nations. Beginning, if one wishes, with *Lysistrata*, Aristophanes could make fun of war as a dangerous and bloody game among men that women sought to put to an end by withholding their sexual favours. This was not merely an entertainment, which still moves audiences to laugh thousands of years after it was written, but also a deep and abiding affirmation of life, against the notion that death somehow can be honourable or glorious in an occupation, namely war, which offers no ready answer to the problems it may be waged to solve. One rebel thinker defined war as a 'socially organized activity for introducing sharp pieces of steel into the bodies of young men'.

Indeed, every culture and every great world religion has a strand in it which emphasizes that which is common between us, that which is peaceful between us, that which is a dialogue between us and can be used in the place of hostility and aggression. It is unnecessary here to recall the importance of peace both inside ourselves and in the world around us to the founders of the world's great religions.

Later, on an intellectual and secular basis, war would be questioned for the waste of young lives, the sacking of great cities and the loss of great cultural memories and histories by many who either were students of the past or were attempting to understand the present dynamics of their societies. Avatars of the culture of peace include thinkers from every region of the world. Gandhi represented not only his own rootedness in his own Asian culture but significant youthful experience in South Africa and Great Britain. Others who understood the price paid for a culture of war were often those who had directly experienced combat and its costs. The great American general, William Tecumseh Sherman, who led his army through Georgia to defeat the Confederacy, became even more famous for the phrase, 'War is hell.' Similarly, the trench poets who chronicled the British experience of the First World War, Robert Graves, Siegfried Sassoon, Wilfred Owen and Rupert Brooke, developed metaphors for mass violence never before used in formal English. George Grosz's drawing of Christ on a cross with a gas mask is part of a figurative pacifist tradition that includes the work of Goya and Picasso.

By the end of the Second World War, artists and writers, academics and politicians were ready to explore a multilateral vision of a potential culture of peace. Meeting in London throughout much of the war, they were conscious that the 1920s and the 1930s had witnessed a paroxysm of militarism, in part caused by the intense experience of the trenches. Italian Fascism taught children in the primary grades to recite 'Obey, believe, fight.' German children of the 1930s were taught by the National Socialists to 'think with their blood' and a Nazi slogan proclaimed, 'Whenever I hear the word "culture" … I release the safety catch on my pistol.'

UNESCO, created in London in 1946 against this background, has continually sought to 'build the defences of peace in the minds of men'. This hope that tolerance and dialogue could gently conjure away violence remains the core ethical mission of the organization. Despite the intervening tensions of cold war and nuclear stalemate, UNESCO and all its supporters throughout the world – teachers, scientists, writers, journalists and artists – have sought to advance the culture of peace through education, culture, science and communication. These activities of the human intellect are understood as the windows onto a more tolerant and civilized future. They form the aesthetics of a reachable Utopia against the background of potential dystopia.

Thus the events of the recent past have removed many of the ideological obstacles to a more pertinent and concrete international cooperation in intellectual matters. The visionaries of the 1940s could perhaps never have imagined that their brief, hopeful world could be recaptured and relived 40 years later. Yet these were patient and persistent, even practical, dreamers.

My own early childhood in Barcelona was marked by civil war. My adolescence and adulthood were lived under the shadow of hot war and cold war on the European continent. As a scientist, I have dedicated my research interests to ensuring the proper development of the brain in the newborn child. As an educator, I have worked to win political space for academic freedom and the social responsibility of the university in different political contexts. As a committed citizen, I participated in my country's transition to democracy. In all of this I try to express my deep conviction that violence is never inevitable and that the culture of war need not last beyond its time. Instability theory teaches us that we must not only expect the unexpected but that we must act in a timely fashion to prevent catastrophes from becoming inevitable. It also teaches us that, in human affairs, events can move at unexpectedly rapid rhythms and that we must adapt to that pace or be left behind.

2 Individuals or Persons

The individual is often an abstraction in certain concepts of the life of people in society. The individual is frequently presented as a consumer, as a passive viewer of the media, as a predictable, statistical abstract of a larger group. Yet that notion of an individual somehow cut off from others, somehow denuded of a personality and feelings and aspirations is, I believe, a very poor basis for understanding the nature of community. Each child, from the moment of birth, is extremely dependent on others and yet each child carries with him or herself a set of potentials and genetic inheritances which make that child an utterly unique addition to the human species. We know, all too well, that a child deprived of warmth and emotion and nurture, in short deprived of the support of the family, either nuclear or extended, is a child who will survive damaged into adolescence and adulthood. And so it is that, in imagining people as relatively empty or relatively abstract individuals, we misperceive those who make up society as being without basic needs, including affective needs, and without deeply held beliefs, aesthetics and dreams.

No matter where we are, or how mature we believe we have become, none of us really lives entirely alone as an individual cut off from others. John Donne wrote, 'No man is an island.' What I believe he meant and what I believe the concept of identity adds to our understanding of the mere individual, is that we come into our professional and educational lives carrying a set of beliefs, tastes and concerns which have come from our interaction with others. This is not only a set of others which we could define as our parents, or our grandparents, but a much broader range of persons who have influenced us with their ideas, their teaching, their art, their symbols – all of which have had an impact on the kind of person we have become. By defining ourselves merely as individuals, we tend to avoid the responsibility that comes with the sovereignty of being a living and growing person.

'The individual' is too often used as an abstract for the anonymous, for those without fame or repute, for those who have made their contributions to life but whose contributions are often not valued at that person's own level and therefore the personal identity of the so-called individual is lost. That loss is in our failure to remember those who have preceded us, those who have contributed to make our life what it is today. An example of historical abstraction which sees our predecessors as having guided us towards being members of an undifferentiated mass, is our present-day concern for the global environment. Untold numbers of scientists have laboured in their laboratories studying the sea coasts or the atmosphere or observing other phenomena around them. Each, as a person, as one committed to advancing our present understanding of the crisis we face in changes in the environment and in our climate, has made a contribution. No-one who pursues knowledge, no-one who shares it, no-one who acquires it by incredible efforts in places where society is so poor that schooling is very difficult to obtain, no one of these persons is merely an individual in a mass. Each of them has an identity and a sovereignty which is a contribution to bettering the human potential.

If we imagine the individual as a matchstick figure standing alone on a white sheet of paper with a circle around it, then we can get a sense of how modern society, urban society, may deprive us of the sense that what we do may very well count, not only for those around us but for many more throughout the world. That sense of being alone in an environment which is not entirely of our making may make us feel that we are not responsible for what happens after us or during our lifetime. Being bombarded with television, radio and press reports on human suffering thousands of kilometres away, may give us the impression that our compassion has been exhausted, so that we cannot respond to the suffering of another individual who is also a person. The notion that we are merely an individual in a world so big, made up of so many institutions and so many movements that our own contribution can only be very small is a demoralizing concept which does not help us form communities of sovereign, active, questing persons who are achieving or trying to achieve goals.

Thus the anonymous nature of that matchstick figure on the page cannot really be us. We know the warp and woof of our lives. Most of us understand that we are part of a 'great chain of being' in which we take what has been given us by generations before and try, in however humble a way, to pass something on to generations in the future. By that very sense of historical time, of our lives being a kind of focus from the past, through the present, to the future, we take on a sense of identity which ultimately involves a question of time.

There is a dictum which holds that it is a curse 'to live in interesting times'. I do not agree. Interesting times are times in which we can test that which makes us persons. They stretch our personalities to become better human beings with greater potentials and more open approaches to all the textures and challenges of the world around us. They call upon us to stretch our perceptions beyond the immediate and the personal to the world as a whole. Having a sense of our own identity should help us to conceptualize what it must be like to be a street child in a Latin American city, a peasant in a drought-ridden part of Asia, or a young girl abandoned to the vice and degradation of life in industrialized parts of the world. Knowledge of ourselves as persons teaches us that we can come together, interact and make efforts as groups, as communities, to tackle, to understand and solve the problems of our time. It teaches us that we are part of a family of man rather than isolated, alone and helpless.

Perhaps it would be better were we to understand ourselves as groups of figures, talking to each other, thinking problems through with each other, doing research together, rather than as isolated, encapsulated individuals cut off from others. For it is with others, and through and from others, that we can develop a sovereignty and an active voice in the world which can enable our lives to contribute to the lives of those around us and those yet to come. I am reminded from my travels in some of the poorest countries of the world of classrooms without blackboards or chalk, in which a single teacher with many, many children gives the best of him or herself to bring them to the magic of the written word, to become literate and participant in a world much broader than their own locality. On one such visit I was introduced as 'Professor Mayor' and I turned to the young schoolmaster in his little hut and said: 'I was Professor Mayor when entering here. I leave as Mr Mayor, without my title. You are the professor and I admire your work.' Thus we must transcend titles and transcend our local setting in order to grasp both intellectually and emotionally the things that are happening in the world around us.

In this I am also mindful of the 800 million people in the world, each of them a person who cannot read, who cannot write, who very often lives on the very margin of absolute poverty. Their identity is invested in survival and the best in them is often never fully developed or touched or reached so that each could contribute to what is a human project of this century and beyond: a greater quality of life for all. That is why it is my experience that no-one should be written off or rejected because of their lack of opportunity or because of the misuse of opportunities at any point in their lives. I believe that within all of us are a number of potential personas that we can develop, nurture and strengthen, so that each of us becomes a potential contributor, even a potential leader, in the communities in which we live and in which we hope to make our contributions. Thus education in its broadest sense is a way in which each of us as an individual can develop into a person, a contributor, a truth-seeker, a truth-teller who can, quite unconsciously, help each community and each society move towards a better existence.

In this I am particularly concerned to begin the process of nurturing the best in each of us, in each of our persons, from earliest childhood. Consider the enormous social and economic waste of the child born brain-damaged because of insufficient nutrition or maternal care during gestation. Consider the enormous potential waste of the human genetic wealth in these children who, with our present-day knowledge, could be born as normal, growing and fully capable persons. If we can imagine the amount of investment put into the intensive care unit of many hospitals, why cannot we understand that the simplest requirements of nutrition and care can ensure that subnormal or retarded children can be prevented in so many cases? This is something in which we have failed, as societies and communities, to look at the very basic building-blocks of our communities. Infant care and nutrition, prenatal and perinatal care and nutrition are all factors which make it possible for persons to be full contributors throughout their lives to the world around us. This is in no way to deny identity to the child born with some damage. Very often, with proper treatment and proper education, such children have wonderful and exceptional gifts to offer us.

Thus a new concept of identity in the circumstances of our present century would require us to understand better the options available to our communities, and to ourselves as members of communities, to act against things which are *never* inevitable. No one of us can simply walk away from the greenhouse effect or from the risks of war and its human and environmental aftermath.

As a research scientist specializing in the development of the brain, a biochemical speciality, I have been privileged to study and to understand how much we develop as persons inside the womb. The accession to becoming a person, in other words the expression of both genetic and environmental elements, inside us and outside us, is an extremely complicated and rich process. It begins very early and, I would add, our development as persons is a lifelong project. We perhaps quest and learn more as children than we do as adults. The ability of a child to perceive and understand such concepts as up and down, light and dark, or hunger and being satisfied is part of an enormous learning process that occurs in a very short space of time. Moreover, that learning, with proper love and nurture, happens outside any institutionalized setting and is a tribute to the sensory and analytic capacities of the human brain. It is also a tribute to teachers who, in the first stages of our life, are almost always our mothers. Mothers carry an enormous responsibility in introducing the young child to the world of the most basic kinds of learning. It is they who with love, tenderness and perseverance are the first teachers and remain, as the child grows, a teacher in the most basic sense of one who provides learning with support.

Support, in this sense, means an emotional bond which allows the learner to feel that sharing, questioning or analysing is being done in a context of concern for the free development of a person.

Urie Bronfenbrenner, the great American specialist on child development, has written and lectured often on the importance of that initial bond between mother and child. All too often, in very large or very poor families, this maternal role is played by older sisters who take on a learning but maternal role, a kind of apprenticeship in which they are the principal caretakers of the very young child. In this interaction, Bronfenbrenner points to the enormous importance of joy and of appreciation from the mother or the primary caretaker toward the infant. As he puts it, in characteristically colloquial English, the mother 'must view that child as the greatest thing since sliced bread'. This means that the child setting out on the road to learning already understands how important he or she is to the person who is with them the most. That child develops a sense of security and self-respect from the joy expressed at its very existence. Of course the family, even in the richest countries, cannot always provide this level of initial security and support, but ideally this is the relationship that creates a learner who will remain open and secure and concerned about the things around him or her for the rest of their lives.

From the scientific perspective, the mother is expressing, consciously or unconsciously, the wonder of the uniqueness of each individual human being. Often it is rightly said that the great monuments of civilization are precious and important to our understanding of ourselves. Places like Moenjodaro or Borobudur or the Pyramids and the Sphinx or Machu Picchu are wonderful reminders of what mankind has been capable of, even in the distant past. But the greatest wonder of the world is the living, unique, human person. Each man, woman and child on this planet represents a new combination of genetic features and, indeed, a new set of human potentials. Moreover, each individual man, woman and child represents, in the present, a set of social and cultural elements which will be passed on to the future and which will manifest themselves in the way they deal with the problems and the challenges of the present.

That is why education in its broadest sense, but also schooling in its most practical sense, is of such basic importance to the development of persons and therefore of their communities. The role of the teacher and particularly the primary schoolteacher in this world is one I can only call heroic and fundamental. It is the primary schoolteacher, who, regardless of the family background or experience of the child, is the opener of the doors to learning and continuing development and education as a human being. It is the teachers, with their warmth and commitment, often in the difficult circumstances I have described above, who can launch a person from a very modest or difficult background towards the heights of knowledge and contribution. And yet our teachers at primary, secondary and sometimes even university levels are ill-paid and often not very respected in their societies. This is another example of a set of values or habits which fly in the face of everything we understand reality to be. We entrust our children to teachers who often, especially in the Third World, have to take on two or more extra jobs simply to make it possible for their own families to survive. Indeed, the debt crisis which is having such a harmful effect on the developing countries, and particularly the poorest among them, has had as one of its first consequences cutbacks in primary and secondary educational opportunities and net reductions in salaries. This, to me, is absurd. We can hardly build a future by economizing on precisely those investments we know build better opportunities for the next generation. Many economists and educational theorists are aware that the great economic miracles of some economies, notably in Asia, are based on enormous investment in primary, secondary and university schooling. Education is not only a human right, it is a positive, proven benefit to society as a whole. Paraphrasing Juan Bautista Alberdi's dictum, we could say: 'To educate is to govern.'

The culture of war has often meant that far more social investment, expenditure and, indeed, respect for certain functions of society go towards military purposes than towards the essential functions of education and teaching. Should we compare the vast amounts of money invested in armaments and military establishments with those invested in the education of our young, I am afraid that the results would indicate that our priorities have gone in a rather odd direction. I am of course mindful that, in our present-day world with its welcome trends towards disarmament and greater international understanding, armies and military establishments still have their place and their roles to perform. However, those roles must be seen against the perspective of the basic needs of children and the ability to provide the widest possible range of educational opportunities for people of all ages. That is why it is particularly worrying that hundreds of millions of people have never had the opportunity to learn to read or write and that tens of millions of children in the Third World never get to attend a primary school. This is, to me, a remarkable disinvestment in the future. The primary school, with its initial learning tools, can prepare someone, even in a society with relatively limited resources for education and other development priorities, to become a learner for a whole lifetime.

Thus a modest investment in expanding primary school systems could lead to a greater degree of learning, of self-awareness and of social participation in the work of development and in the work of building a better community. Indeed, by 1991–2, UNESCO's educational statistics were showing, for the first time, a *decline* in the absolute number of illiterates throughout the world. Much remains to be done, but we should be encouraged by the fact that every day there are fewer illiterates than there were yesterday.

From this approach to the whole person it is important to draw some conclusions about the priorities that should be adopted concerning the educational and cultural environment in which we prepare the next generation. We exist in space and time. We inhabit localities and communities with local problems and local issues towards whose resolution the efforts of each of us are required. We also inhabit a blue and green planet with its life-support systems which have so far served us very well, but we are now in a relationship with nature which seems to be turning hostile. Man, who felt himself capable of mastering nature, is now beginning to understand that the very weight of his population on the planet and its use of such things as fossil fuels and wood burning and pollutants and other materials have stretched our life-support systems perhaps to the limit. Part of being a person is to understand that we are natural creatures, dependent on nature, in interaction with nature, and therefore we must begin to develop a new perception and respect for the limits of what we can do to nature.

And yet, even at the top of the educational and social pyramid, in even the richest societies, we have a tendency to isolate ourselves in our narrow specialities or our daily occupations and forget our linkages with others around the world and that enormous set of human interactions with nature which threaten the survival of our species. Traditional education carries with it the risk of transforming open and aware young students into narrow-minded citizens, out of touch with society and the important issues of their times. Here we must think very carefully about the values that are taught even at the highest levels of education – about what we are to do in our professional and private lives as people with a great deal of training and a great deal of social influence. I like to say over and over again that the scientist has an absolute responsibility to speak out on the issues he knows about, on the issues he studies and which can affect public well-being. I have always felt that the university and other intellectual fora should encourage scientists and scholars in many other disciplines to express themselves in public in such a way as to inform the debate on such issues as environment or development or, for that matter, the development and nurturing of democratic institutions. Yet our specialities have been taught in ways which define us into narrow boxes, often with language or jargon or ways of approaching matters which are cut off from specialists just around the corner in the next academic department. Thus specialization can be seen as a way of removing us from the responsibilities of being persons and moulding us into a kind of predictable and passive individual who views the world from his ivory tower. This must stop. An ivory tower is not a point from which the problems of the modern world can be addressed. We cannot look on as mere spectators of the playing out of forces which may determine the lives of our children and their children in a measurable space of future time.

Here I come to one of the main problems of the modern world, bureaucracy. Our complex civilizations, in the cities both of the industrialized and of the developing worlds, have been based on a sense of specialization, hierarchy and discipline. There is nothing wrong with these values, properly applied. But they are improperly applied when people with knowledge and skill in certain areas find themselves incapable of freely expressing their views, which may disagree with the dominant 'wisdom' of their social milieu. Bureaucracy can often act as a limitation on our being a fully developed person. By existing with a set of assigned roles, we may limit ourselves to a routine set of activities and forget that we do exist in a broader world in which each of us has a responsibility to make a contribution. I have often said that I admire good bureaucrats. By that I mean that the good bureaucrat is one who keeps a complex organization functioning well. By functioning well I mean that the organization and the individual both show a capacity to learn and to grow. This of course is not the standard model of bureaucracy as we know it in our time.

All too often, the successful career takes place within a bureaucracy. The university is also a form of bureaucracy, as are the great international and national – public and private – bureaucracies that influence so much in our lives. Inside them we may have lost that most important set of characteristics which makes an individual into a growing and sensitive person. This may shock and upset, but careful thought on the subject leads me to believe that the most important quality in developing into a person who can contribute to the world around us is the capacity not to conform; it is the capacity to raise serious questions about what is considered ordinary or normal around us and, above all, it is the capacity to take risks. We must all learn to transcend specialization, the bureaucratic definitions that often narrow us down to being less than we are. We must guard against the tunnel vision which tells us we cannot look beyond what we are supposedly assigned by society, business or bureaucracy as our jobs. All of us are alive, sentient and feeling beings with many personal options within us. It is for us and the structures together to potentiate what is the best in us so that it can be expressed in democratic and spontaneous ways.

What does this mean in actuality? From my perspective as a former rector of a university, and as the director-general of an international organization, with a broad mandate, it means that we must develop within our children and within ourselves a capacity to go against the things which seem so ordinary and natural, and so acceptable in our environment, both natural and social. It means that we should feel very strongly and deeply when a child is suffering on the other side of the world. It means that we should feel a sense of outrage when institutions and governments cannot agree on ways to develop peaceful procedures for solving international problems. It means that we should give great respect to the teachers among us, especially to the humble village teachers of the poorest countries who work so hard and make such sacrifices to build the future.

It also means that we must fight against our own laziness and our own socially trained propensity to conform and to be quiet. We should all be, in the best of democratic settings, a bit of a rebel. We should be able to mobilize what we have to say and what we know, to partici-pate in the social debates of our time and not simply stand aside and let things go on as they are. I do not believe in 'business as usual' in a world where population, ignorance and poverty are growing to the point where they will threaten the security of those of us in even the richest countries. We cannot ignore the fundamentalist impulse and the violent predilections which take root in situations of hopelessness and despair, when poverty seems to have no solutions. We cannot ignore the fact that the greenhouse effect and other environmental issues have profound impacts on our ability to feed our children, on our ability to go on with our civilization as defined in its best sense. We cannot permit 'business as usual' or old habits to prevail.

Earlier in this chapter, I spoke about the important role of mothers. For the moment I would like to share the importance of fathers, who often bear the burden of seeing to it that a family survives in very difficult circumstances. I am mindful, in the life of my own generation and in my own life, of the remarkable role of my own father in giving me an example of one who goes against the probabilities in order to succeed in making a contribution to society. He was an extremely modest manual worker in the town of Tortosa in Catalonia. He first earned his living by cleaning windows, but he moved to Barcelona and began to work in business, again at a very modest level. He was penniless and without much in the way of education or background. Yet he succeeded in becoming the manager of a number of shoe shops in the city. At the end of the Second World War, he risked the family savings and the family's well-being in an enormous risk. He established Spain's first penicillin factory and built it with great care and courage into a major enterprise. So confident was he of his abilities to manage this kind of pharmaceutical business that when a large firm offered to buy him out he calmly turned to them and said, 'In a number of years, it will be my firm who will buy you out.' This was, in fact, what happened. In a very personal way, my father is a kind of rebel, one who has not accepted destiny or the future as something decided ahead of time.

It has not been an easy life for him. During the Spanish civil war he was jailed by the Republicans for being a Catholic and jailed by the Nationalists for being a Republican. And yet he persevered in his business career and in his concern for his family, to the point that one must say that he has led a most successful life. To this day he remains dedicated to the notion that one can do whatever has to be done if one can take the necessary risks and make the necessary sacrifices. This is both an old-fashioned and very modern view of what a person is. In my own life this was brought home to me very dramatically when, at a very young age, I was named Rector of the University of Granada, far to the south of my native region of Spain. This ancient and venerable institution, founded in 1517, was located in a province with enormous problems of poverty. Granada had one of the highest levels of malnutrition in new-born infants. As a scientist specializing in the brain biochemistry of infants and as one with a commitment to work for retardation prevention I was most disturbed to discover that the university, its teachers and its students were cut off from the life of the city around them. I therefore decided that the university would meet its responsibilities to its urban community.

Post-natal analysis facilities were made available to the poorest areas and specialized clinical services for expectant mothers were established. By providing good nutritional and medical advice free of charge, these facilities were able to lower the retardation rate in Granada dramatically over a very short period of time. Ultimately, this led to a national policy on the matter which prevented much preventable retardation at very low cost, a very small investment in time and effort by specialists. It is perhaps worth mentioning that these efforts by one university towards its community took place before Spain had made its transition to democracy, when such efforts by a university were viewed with more suspicion than they would have been within a framework of public freedom. And yet I felt that the university and its personnel, and particularly its students, had a responsibility to make a difference in its setting. We were not merely at the university in order to advance ourselves and advance our knowledge, but rather we were also there to share our knowledge with those around us. Much later, after I was elected Director-General of UNESCO, I was lecturing in the University of Madrid and I read a poem of the Catalan poet Jesus Massip, which can be translated as follows:

> When the hours come back
> they will find us already settled and docile
> ('LLibre d'hores', Tortosa, Spain, 1990)

I ended by saying: 'Mr Rector, I hope that we will never be docile. The university must never be docile. We must be the institution that provides the decision makers with scientific elements and asks the questions that perhaps upset those around us but must be asked none the less.'

Docility, passivity, a sense of being a spectator, are all perhaps results of a culture which turns us into recipients of information and passive witnesses to problems that seem to be insoluble. This is far from the case. I believe that all of us have a role to play and that many of the problems around us need only to be fully felt and experienced in order to lead us to act in order to find solutions.

It is true that normal life, particularly in the modern world, does indeed tend to isolate and deresponsibilize. Partly this is the fault of bureaucratic organizations, partly it is the fault of highly-specialized professional lives. But it is also our own fault. We have the ability to reach beyond the barriers of ourselves and our localities and to see and analyse and, yes, to *feel* the suffering of those not so far away or very far away which can be solved, which can be avoided.

Ultimately, we come back to the core of ethical beliefs according to which our lives should be led. We have been taught this fundamental set of, if not rules, at least guides to existence by our religious beliefs, by our philosophical training and by our professional development in all the levels of our lives from the moment we were born through our full educational and experiential development into adulthood. Yet somehow, at certain stages of the development of many, that ethical core is lost to indifference or to a sense that nothing can really be accomplished for a better life, for a better human quality of life. Too often, we feel we must scramble and compete with others in order to advance ourselves at their cost.

This is the cynical wisdom of the culture of war. This is the individual as warrior armed against others in the Hobbesian universe of the war of all against all. It is a world defined as so insecure and threatening that 'order' requires absolute power on the part of the rulers and absolute obedience on the part of the ruled. Otherwise life would be 'nasty, brutish and short'. That is not our world, nor was it the world of even Hobbes's time if one accepts his opponent's critique of Hobbesian logic. John Locke argued that life could be enhanced by a set of contractual and more or less democratic community arrangements among people. Hobbes, I would argue, with great respect for his intellect, was a spokesman for a culture of war that came out of the trauma of the English civil strife of the 17th century. Locke was one of the avatars of the notion of a culture of peace and community responsibility for the betterment of each member. Locke, by the way, has been shown, through the developments of modern science, to be one of the most astute observers of the educational process.

We are faced with an enormous change in our behaviour and in our attitudes. As we near the end of this bloody and often horrifying century, we have already seen that a great number of people could come together and tear down the Berlin wall. We have seen the 'velvet revolution' of Czechoslovakia and the other relatively bloodless revolutions that brought down totalitarian political systems that seemed destined to survive for many years to come. We are privileged witnesses to the acts of communities in striving continually and successfully towards freedom. We forget, very often, here in the industrialized West, that these people have come through a long tunnel of oppression and suffering to emerge into the light of freedom. Success came after years of patient and often very risky efforts to combat a system that had all the power on its side. Here it is worthwhile to recall that the President of the Czech Federal Republic, Vaclav Havel, has been in and out of jail almost continuously under the previous system. Yet he has emerged as a thoughtful, young, uncynical leader towards the future. In this, he represents the best in what art and culture can contribute to us as persons and to communities building democracy. For democracy fundamentally is the respect for each and every person in our environment and, even more important, the respect for ourselves as persons with rights and with responsibilities for what goes on around us.

For all the reasons, implicit and explicit, written above, emphasizing the person as opposed to the individual, I have decided to launch UNESCO on a new path, in education in particular. Almost 20 years ago, UNESCO produced perhaps its best known work on education, the book *Learning To Be*. It was drafted by a commission of leading scholars and educationists under the chairmanship of former French Prime Minister and Education Minister, Edgar Faure. *Learning To Be* remains one of the great pioneering works of education, pointing towards new ways of opening the human mind through new and more interactive methods of education from primary to university level. It remains very relevant to the educational world of today.

Yet I believe that our needs as we move towards the next century require that we add to *Learning To Be* a new and even more basic notion of humanity that should suffuse the educational system and indeed suffuse our communities. That concept is something I call 'learning to care'. This means giving and sharing. On his small work table, Abbé Pierre – for more than 40 years, France's conscience on poverty and homelessness – has a slip of paper with the inscription: 'There is only one pressing need – sharing'. When that happens, individuals are persons. They are not merely counted. They count.

Learning to care means that the educational curriculum should include within it all the due respect and attention we need to create and nurture altruism within our children and within ourselves. Altruism is a very difficult concept to describe in purely rational or clinical terms, but it means that ability to think beyond one's immediate needs or one's immediate desires in order to act with a great deal of love and respect for all those in our environment. It means the capacity to transcend the narrowness of locality or of speciality to reach out and make a contribution towards the world.

Thus to me and, I hope, to those who will support these efforts, learning to care would be a way of building in the school those fundamental ethical values which have been the touchstones of so much of what is beautiful and creative in community life. Learning to care means first of all caring for ourselves. By caring for ourselves I mean instilling that sense of dignity and self-respect from which all other acts in society become possible. Learning to care also means caring about the natural environment and our role in it. It means that we must all have a certain degree of scientific or ecological literacy so that we can understand the trends in the environment which have the very real potential to threaten or disrupt our present way of life. After all, if the greenhouse effect trends continue, it seems clear that the only way to confront them will involve fairly profound changes in the way we live. It means that caring about nature would have to be translated into very concrete decisions and actions by all of us. It means using artificial fertilizers only when no alternative is available; it means burning less fossil fuels; it means finding other ways of producing energy; it means thinking about investment in a much different time frame than the immediate here and now. Thus, in learning to care about nature and then in learning to care about and tolerate the differences and circumstances of others, we can become active citizens of our communities, indeed of the broader, global community, in ways which can lead to solutions of problems. To a significant extent this also means caring enough about each individual life on the planet so that we can never fall victim to what some call 'compassion fatigue' and which supposedly involves that tiredness of the moral fibre, that apathy or indeed anomie that audiences sometimes seem to manifest when exposed over and over again to images of starvation and suffering, particularly in the poorest countries of the world. Compassion is not something which should ever grow tired. I believe that it can remain active and alert when compassion is expressed in acts which seek to solve problems. Rather than merely observing or feeling, however important those first acts are, we must always be prepared to move on and seek mechanisms and solutions to poverty and to suffering in the here and now.

To learn to care from the earliest age requires deeply caring family structures and/or educational structures that can emphasize the need to see and feel what goes on around us by making us feel that we can make a difference. And here I come back to Urie Bronfenbrenner's interaction of mother and child. Somehow – and our best teachers know how to do this – we must create a generation of teachers, particularly at primary levels (but, it is hoped, going up all the way to the most difficult specialities) who make the link between the body of knowledge covered and the level of ethical responsibility owed to the world in general. José Martí, poet and father of Cuban independence, once wrote: 'When a child is born, he has a right to be educated. Once grown, it is his duty to educate others.' No knowledge, however obscure, should be left outside the education process.

I have never believed that by being a biochemist I have given up my right to try to be a poet or to be a politician. I feel that I have many facets that I must express and even test in order to find the combination of skills and sensitivities that could make me the person that I wish to be. That is why, when I awaken each morning and see the sun rise, I try to imagine the child thousands of kilometres away at daybreak, sunset or in the dark who is hungry, who may never get an education, who may never in fact survive the night. I constantly try to remind myself of the suffering I have seen. This is not a pleasant exercise but life is not entirely a pleasant or pain-free experience. Life requires an enormous amount of caring even towards those people far removed from our immediate surroundings and experience.

Learning to care is based on this belief: that each of us must take into ourselves the problems, absurdities and contradictions of what goes on around us and that we must feel a certain degree of passion to change them. In that sense, the best guarantee of the development of democracy, not only at local and national levels but throughout the world, is the fact that we must all to some extent be rebels, but rebels with a cause. And so I recently wrote as part of a poem:

> Are you complaining
> about the strong surge of feeling?
> For that we want
> the bravery
> of those who do not accept
> merely
> the visible.
>
> Calm is submission,
> depression,
> death.
>
> Life
> is in the whirl
> where the wind lashes
> and each cell shakes
> and believes
> in the impossible.
>
> Only rebels
> are beacons
> for the change
> that the human condition
> demands.

3   E Pericoloso Sporgersi!: Leaning and Learning

In developing as persons we are continually confronted by the problem of perspective. Perspective results from that set of perceptual lenses and categories that we develop from education systems, from our social environment, from our families – in short from our biographies in a given place and time. So all-encompassing are these perspectives that they form a kind of theatrical set to everything else that we do. They influence, without our necessarily knowing it, our ways of viewing and even understanding new facts that present themselves in our lives and in the times we live in.

Perception is a reality, in the sense that it is the grid and the matrix through which the world tries to speak to us, but it is also the limit and sometimes the obstacle that keeps our minds and our feelings from fully grasping what goes on about us. Perception is also an academic field of study. A number of most enlightening experiments have been carried out on perception by behavioural scientists. Perhaps the most interesting was the set of experiments carried out by Leo Festinger at Stanford in the early 1960s, which led to the development of the theory of cognitive dissonance. Festinger and his team of researchers provided students, selected on the basis of their religious or ideological backgrounds, with lists of facts which they were to note on a questionnaire. The team working at Stanford discovered that students with very strong religious or ideological backgrounds simply did not see facts that contradicted the beliefs they had grown up with. Thus the mind is more than a passive receiver, according to this theory. Rather, the mind projects any number of interferences with facts and experiences in the world around it. We can, in fact, 'tune out' sets of information which might be essential to our intellectual or emotional growth. Thus being a person requires a continual level of effort to evaluate and understand the perceptual scheme we have developed out of our lives or the perceptual scheme we have inherited from our culture or our academic speciality. This, of course, brings us back to the most basic of philosophical propositions, namely that the unexamined life is not worth living. A constant process of self-examination and self-doubt is in fact the scientific stance we have come to expect in the physical and social sciences, along with the critical attitude which helps us advance in the humanities. The trained scientist, like the trained observer in other fields, is therefore called upon consistently to root about in the intellectual baggage he or she carries around and to look at many of the items in there and decide whether they still belong.

On many trains, particularly in Europe, a sign is prominently displayed by each window. It reads: 'E pericoloso sporgersi – Es peligroso asomarse al exterior – Ne pas se pencher dehors – Nicht hinauslehnen – Don't lean out'. But to see the train that we are on – our culture, our background, our institutional setting – we should not lean too far in. We should be prepared at times to lean out in order to see what it is that is carrying us along the tracks. If we withdraw too far inside we become lost in the accepted wisdom of our speciality, of our institution and of our culture. It is sometimes worth the risk of leaning as far out as we possibly can in order to look back at the train that carries us and decide, from a more objective perspective, whether it is going in the right direction. In fact, to be rebels with a cause we even question the tracks on which we roll, because those we perceive or think are correct may in fact be leading in a direction set so long ago in the past that they no longer correspond to present needs. It was Thomas Huxley, grandfather of UNESCO's first director-general, Julian Huxley, who wrote in 1893: 'Social progress means a checking of the cosmic process at every step and the substitution for it of another which may be called the ethical process.'

Checking the cosmic process has become a matter of acute scientific and political concern in today's world. International meetings have been held over the last year or so on such specific aspects of the environment as acid rain, ozone layer depletion, the transport of waste and global warming trends. My concern is that, from a scientific perspective, and from urgent world policy needs, each of these issues relates to the broader issue of human interaction with the environment. These are interrelated phenomena requiring a holistic approach to attaining better and more precise knowledge of ecological trends and taking urgent and often simple measures to begin to confront them. Moreover, we exist in a world with an ever-widening gap between those with wealth and industrial and agricultural capacity and those with a steadily diminishing capacity to cope with the needs of development.

This is not a very attractive vision of the present or of the next century. Nor is it something which should lead us into passivity or defeatism. This should be emphasized time and again. It should, however, strengthen our resolve to meet 'intergenerational responsibilities'. I do not speak here only of generations yet to come or even of our grandchildren. I speak also of our children now, because another perspective and another perceptual issue concern time and the way in which we must make decisions to cope with the present. Instability theory, to which I have already referred, teaches, in the words of Ilya Prigogine, the Nobel chemistry laureate, that time has returned to the practice and understanding of science. If events move at an unsteady pace which can accelerate and which can reach a point of no return, beyond which little can be done to prevent a process from turning to catastrophe, then we must take time very seriously indeed. We must understand that the flow of time and human and natural events could carry us along passively if we do not learn to act quickly and appropriately even in the absence of complete information. Hegel warned us that 'fear of making mistakes is in itself a mistake since it can be seen as being fear of the truth'.

One of the main problems of the 20th century, according to Bertrand Russell, is the need to make decisions in the absence of full information. That is a very human and a very intellectual responsibility which cannot be postponed. If we do not act 'in time', future generations will have no time to act at all: they may be the hostages to processes gone out of control. Those processes could be environmental trends in which the very weight of human population on the planet has pushed natural conditions beyond the point where they can support life; or the equally human problem of dividing the world into a very small and wealthy area in the north and an incredibly explosive and expanding area of absolute poverty in the south.

The need for action, a sense of urgency, can only be created when we learn to 'lean out' and understand other countries, other cultures and other people. Learning to care requires textbooks and teachers who can relate our national histories to the cultures and achievements of distant countries. A global vision of humanity, in all its many cultural forms, should be provided from the earliest years of schooling. It requires newspapers and electronic media that report the news from other societies and other regions of the world with the same urgency as they cover local and national events. Similarly, political decision making should be based on a global, holistic approach to problems with due attention to the most up-to-date scientific knowledge and to the experiences of other governments confronting the same range of problems.

Each of these changes in perspective would help citizens to transcend their local settings, break out of routine ways of thinking about 'others' and learn to care. To grasp our contemporary world fully, we must follow the words of the famous tango of Eladia Blazquez, heard beautifully sung by Susana Rinaldi, 'Tengo el corazon mirando al sur'. Our perspective should 'look to the south' and cross the great divide of rich and poor on the planet.

The Berlin wall has come down. Yet stronger and wider walls deep within ourselves continue to divide us from others. Before us now is the seemingly fantastic but truly possible task of demolishing the walls in our minds. Together we can change our attitudes and habits. Together we can prevent the fortification of the wall between the world's north and south. That is why I hope in years to come we will have discovered ways and means of reaching those people living in villages who today are still isolated from the modern communications network and unaware of what is happening in the world around them. At the other end of the economic scale, we must also reach those who occupy the world's executive suites and who are so rooted in institutions, routines and bureaucracy that they can no longer see the human dilemmas and dramas that go on about them even within a few miles of their place of business.

In a set of experiments that were as important and pathbreaking in behavioural psychology as Festinger's, a team at Yale University, under Professor Stanley Milgrim, studied authority and the capacity of individuals to inflict pain on others. The so-called 'Milgrim experiments' were based on the conundrum of understanding how mass violence could be perpetrated by ordinary people during the holocaust of the Second World War. In fact, the laboratory was decorated with the famous photograph of the soldier whose feet were dangling over a trench full of bodies, with a cigarette held nonchalantly to his lips and a machine-gun lying casually on his lap. At the beginning of the experiments the team predicted that only 10 per cent of the subjects would go in the direction of overt violence towards another person, but, as in the biological and genetic approaches that were so important to the Seville Statement on violence, it was established by this psychological experiment that social and cultural factors could lead in the direction of unexpected human behaviour. There are no excuses: as Article I of the Universal Declaration of Human Rights states, 'All human beings are born free and equal'. We cannot look to genetics for help in explaining violence and oppression:

> Men at some time are masters of their fates:
> The fault, dear Brutus, is not in our stars,
> But in ourselves, that we are underlings.
> (Shakespeare, *Julius Caesar*)

Men are not born violent. They are made so: made oppressive, unequal and aggressive, caught in the tangle of life.

The Milgrim experiments involved a drama student in a chair and a kind of radio control room which the subject entered with a white-coated scientist. The subject was asked to continually 'raise the voltage' as the actor in the 'electrified' chair 'failed' to answer a set of questions correctly. Given calm and authoritative instructions to increase the voltage at each so-called 'error' made by the actor in the chair, the vast majority of subjects raised the voltage to the highest point. The team's prediction was based on the percentage of mentally ill individuals in any random population. Although the subjects were generally 'healthy', only very few refused to follow orders.

The conclusion of the Milgrim experiments was that inherited authority patterns in our culture and in our society could be used to instil violence in normally very responsible people. The subjects of the experiment were largely people well known for their calm and rigour: the actuaries of the insurance industry located near the campus of Yale University.

Thus our perspectives must be worked on and expanded to encompass what is within us and outside us, better to understand what we can do and where we can situate our priorities. In fact, the dynamics of the experiment were such that the subjects did not lean out of the context of the university, the scientist in his white coat and the notion of authority that led them to perform acts they would not normally have undertaken. Leaning out is an act of rebellion. It is an act of questioning our deepest assumptions about ourselves and our relationship to others and the world and also a way of questioning objectively a number of propositions about the world which we may have learned in the course of our lifetime.

Even those at the very apex of their academic or social pyramids, even those with the most specialized of educations, find themselves so immured in their settings, their jargon and their career patterns that they can no longer look out and see – let alone feel – what goes on around them. It is not enough to understand that there is immense poverty in regions to the south of the industrialized countries. How often are we blinded to the immense poverty which can exist just a few hundred metres from where we are. I am reminded here of the remark made by a public health nurse in a major city in a very wealthy country who, in an attempt to convince a commissioner of health that problems of poverty existed very close to the very wealthy quarters of the city, blurted out, 'Mr Commissioner, a hundred yards, not a hundred miles from here, rats are threatening babies.'

The dynamic of leaning out and of avoiding leaning too far into our local and daily routines is something which requires a great deal of energy and discipline but, most important, it requires an understanding of our uniqueness and our enormous potential. Perhaps the dynamics of modern civilization have taught us a level of insensitivity to things going on around us that we must learn to confront and defeat. We cannot consider ourselves ethical or moral persons if we cannot reach beyond the limits of our existence and probe, often with a great deal of pain, into the suffering around us.

Thus it is not enough to be a highly-trained and very productive research scientist. It is not enough to be a highly successful and capable manager. It is essential to be a whole person and a person existing in a civic setting with responsibilities to one's community and to oneself. Leaning out also requires the capacity for political and community leadership: to listen to scientific expertise when enough data have been gathered, to form at least the beginnings of conclusions which may be difficult to take in. Political leadership must be open and alert to the findings of science when those findings require radical and even searing self-evaluation as regards policies and the need for rapid change. I have been dismayed over past months at the slowness with which the machinery in institutions of power, communication and knowledge is moving towards a cooperative effort on such matters as the environment and global poverty. Each speciality has an organizational form, a hierarchy and usually even a hermetic language of its own. It is easier for each specialist or political actor to remain within the field of people with whom he interacts than to step outside and listen to others. Human change is therefore painfully slow, while global change and the political and social problems that we see around us are accelerating and could accelerate beyond our capacity to act upon them.

Denial and inertia are the main human foibles that can contribute to catastrophe. Safe in our daily routines, secure in our titles and prerogatives, too many of us tend to deny that global change is a priority or that poverty is a problem that can threaten our security even here, in the wealthy north. And once the threat appears to take on all the importance it deserves, institutions and governments seem at a loss to move resolutely and swiftly towards action. Part of the reason for this may be that our perceptions, limited by the immediate horizons of private life and economic gain, focus on the short term. The market has taught us, I believe wrongly, that investments should be made and profits taken quickly. We measure our gains by rates calculated on a daily or weekly basis. Rarely does a political or economic institution manage to think seriously about costs to be paid in a decade or two. By then it is often felt that the problem may have to be solved by others – the next generation and perhaps some scientific *deus ex machina*. This is not unlike the very wealthy terminally ill who place their faith in the future by freezing themselves in the present. The most important matters and strategies require a medium-term or even a long-term outlook (cultural, scientific or educational strategies, environmental measures and so on). In these cases, it is essential to go beyond the normal political terms of office: not government agendas but national agendas are required. Therefore, to ensure continuity, pacts between the most important political forces must be achieved.

Culture, in all its richness and diversity, was once defined by a very perceptive anthropologist as 'a conspiracy against death'. Religious feelings of piety towards nature, respect for older generations and responsibility for the young once bound people together in a shared community-wide structure of feelings. Ethical and philosophical values of 'knowing oneself' and commitment to the common good later came to play a similar, secular role of reaching beyond our private selves and our biological lifespans to a larger, human commonweal. Each of these cultural systems gave significance to the humblest life and the smallest everyday acts of living. At their purest and best these religious and ethical traditions were building-blocks of a culture of peace in a world that was, more often than not, at war. In the contemporary world it may have become fashionable to debunk these cultural and ethical traditions as 'myths'. In fact, they require a careful re-evaluation and a reintegration of our behaviour so that these avatars of a culture of peace can once again be given their proper historical role and be seen in the perspective of what they aim towards. They have been vectors towards the possible Utopias of a world which is opening up to us right here at the end of the 20th century.

The ends of the 17th, 18th and 19th centuries were all Promethean eras of re-evaluation and recombination of ideas and experiences lived over centuries fraught with major political and social change. If the end of the 17th century saw the philosophical beginnings of rationalism, in Descartes' dictum, 'I think, therefore I am', at the end of the 18th century the age of enlightenment stated the problem as: 'If I think and therefore I am, why does my political system keep me from thinking and being?' This was the challenge of the rebels of that century. The work of Montesquieu, Voltaire, Diderot and Rousseau in reperceptualizing and reunderstanding the power relationships that prevented the free expression of ideas led to the first experiments in liberalism and democracy. And at the end of the century which preceded our own, Freud, Einstein and others questioned the very nature of being human and the very nature of time and particles and energy in a remarkable burst of thinking and knowledge. It is a colossal pity that the understanding of the unconscious and the understanding of energy should have been eclipsed by the mass outpourings of hysteria crystallized in totalitarian regimes and by the capacity for mass destruction of the human race crystallized in warheads and bombs. The great thinkers were not hoping for that. As the wall came down in Berlin and as, it is hoped, the walls can begin to come down in ourselves and our institutions, then perhaps their insights and their overtures to this century can lead to a new dedication in the next century to a full respect for the multifaceted nature of being human and an equally full respect for the capacities of science and of learning to contribute to a better quality of life for all on this planet.

The precursors of the culture of peace, be they the founders of the major religions or the philosophers of centuries past or the visionaries and dreamers who have marked our trajectory towards new possibilities, shared a very simple, powerful message. They saw the world through the eyes of a child. They saw the world in particular through the eyes of the famous child who noted that the Emperor's new clothes did not exist and that the Emperor was, in fact, quite naked. It is this quality of questioning assumptions, of probing certainties, of resynthesizing the messages of the culture and coming out with other statements of the problem and other potential solutions which are the marks of human creativity. They are, and always will be, points of rebellion. They are, and always will be, acts of leaning out when the sign says 'E pericoloso sporgersi'.

The culture of war teaches that fierce competition and even the Darwinian evolutionary cycle transposed into the business or social world require all progress by a kind of 'nature red in tooth and claw'. It posits a personality type bent on personal aggrandizement at the cost of others rather than personal growth to the benefit of others. It posits violence as part of human nature when in fact violence is something human nature has evolved from a cultural and social perspective. It posits the capacity to commit aggression out of self-interest, rather than the more courageous opening of understanding and tolerance to significant others outside ourselves.

Over most of the post-war era, division of the world into heavily armed ideological and political blocs has not facilitated intellectual dialogue. Indeed, the very culture of war inside each bloc militated against leaning out and trying to see the world as a whole. UNESCO was during this period – and I am sure a study of its archives and programmes would show this – a slight and fragile but effective bridge between isolated worlds caught up in a race to produce higher and more sophisticated forms of destruction. This was the vision of its founders and it was not a vision rooted only in this century. By speaking of the role of the minds of men in erecting the defences of peace, the founders of UNESCO were making a connection with the most fundamental beliefs of the world's great religions. They were positing dialogue and compassion and a civic culture of peace as an antidote to intolerance, rejection and hatred. Their vision has survived. It is crucial in the context of a new opportunity to build a culture of peace and, against the threat of global change and deepening poverty, to recapture the passion and commitment of those who felt so strongly in 1945. In a very real sense, they were rebels against the horrors of their times. They were poets and politicians, schoolteachers and scientists, but they joined together in projecting their hopes to us. In founding UNESCO, the victorious powers of 1945 came together as a humanistic force for the future. They clearly felt that it was in their own interest and that of the world to create 'bridges of understanding' among people with very different ideologies and to create dialogue among those active in advancing science, education, communication and culture, regardless of their apparent differences.

Long before the Beatles, these distinguished diplomats and thinkers were saying that knowing and teaching, seeking and creating were based on a simple commitment: 'All you need is love; love is all you need'. In our own contemporary crisis of global change and development, this means that each and every human being on this planet is directly concerned with the search for answers and solutions. It means that no-one is a spectator of the approaching threat and that everyone has a role to play.

The greenhouse effect is the result of many small acts committed throughout the world. It concerns what we burn, what we burn it for, what forests we cut down and why we do so, as well as a host of related activities carried out every day. Until we change the way we think and act – our perceptions of ourselves and our relationship to nature – global change will persist. Until we see the connections between poverty and population growth, between the daily struggle for survival in the poorest sections of Third-World cities and rural villages and the problems of the environment, we may fail to come up with effective solutions to provide everyone with a chance of sustainable develop-ment in our lifetimes. For sustainable development, using the world's resources with prudence and foresight for the future, is both an approach to global change and an approach to global poverty.

Some of us are in possession of scientific knowledge or community authority which afford us more of an opportunity to act urgently and effectively than is afforded others. Beginning from the basic love we feel for those closest to us and expanding it to a passion for mankind and the Earth, leadership will have to evolve from the private and short-term perceptions we have learned to new notions of a global community and global commons. Educators, scientists, artists and journalists, along with politicians and spiritual leaders, have a crucial role in revi-talizing the ethics of caring and love and setting new agendas for their disciplines and their societies.

One of the pleasures of university teaching, particularly at the level of introductory courses, is to be reminded of one's own youthful outlook by successive new generations of students. They take nothing for granted, accept few assumptions without careful examination and have not yet 'learned' that such and such a speciality is very different from another. They see things as a whole and continue to look for con-nections. For this reason, young people are often challenging and downright rebellious in the face of received wisdom and ideas. At the same time, they are close enough to childhood to value friendship, love and their own inherited or invented communities. They are often 'warmhearted rebels' against cold institutions.

Then, somehow, most of them grow up and become part of those institutions and share in their rituals and routines. They settle into the institutional pace and jargon. In *In nome dei Papa re*, a film written and directed by Luigi Magni, set in the time of Italian unification in the late 19th century, a young Garibaldino railed at traditional authority in the presence of a cardinal. 'What a pity,' said the Cardinal, 'that most of the rebels die at 18, even if nobody kills them'. Giussepe di Lampedusa's *The Leopard* is a longer story with a similar moral. How then do we remain open and sensitive to the world outside our private and professional lives after we too become active adults? There is no absolute formula but I believe that we must cherish the child and youth within us and that we must remain sceptical of the claims of institutions and institutional roles. Every day, the sunrise should also remind us that time is going by and that looming challenges remain unsolved. It is in this form of meditation, connected to the realities lived around us and the forces at work on the planet, that the spark of rebellion, the dreams and generosity are kept alive. It is worthwhile always having on you, or on your desk, a small sheet of paper with a list of those subjects that are really relevant both to yourself and to your functions. It is particularly useful to glance at them when, in stormy moments, you need to differentiate between the important and the merely urgent.

The question remains concerning how to strengthen our ethical, spiritual and intellectual capacity to lean out and to arrive at a global vision for ourselves and how to share it with others. I often stand before distinguished audiences in the world's great capitals, but always, in my mind's eye, I am thinking of those I have met in my travels, who are not there in the great capitals or the centres of learning of the world. I see a village schoolteacher, patiently working with his or her pupils, to teach them to read and write, to add and subtract. I also see the concern of fathers and mothers that their children be better educated, better off and more secure in the necessities of life. I see the more than 600,000 remote rural villages of the world, most of them kilometres away from any telephone or radio, and I am concerned about our capacity to sustain and help them in developing better education and health services. And I see a young man in the urban slums of the north or the south and sense his desperate search for work and the despair that might drive him to drugs. I see the boredom and the untapped energies of the most affluent young who have almost everything while knowing the price of almost nothing. And last, I see a scientist in an ill-equipped laboratory trying to provide his or her country with a scientific and technological basis for development and decision making. These are the people who must stand at the centre of any concept of education on a global basis because they are the world. And this world, this vision is a *gestalt*, a totality, a set of feelings and a total perception, not a mere listing of concepts.

When the day comes that we can learn from them, and they can learn from us in a continuous sharing, we will have overcome the age-old mistrust of the culture of war and set out on the adventure of a culture of peace. This will involve leaning out and making connections for ourselves that bridge humans and nature, town and countryside, time and space, in a new civic culture for the planet. In our mind's eye we will see in those children, young people and adults the connections between the environmental crisis and the debt crisis, between the billions of dollars a year in the net capital outflow from the south to the north and the laboratories and classrooms which may never be built. We need immediate measures before irreversible social and environmental damage is done. It is the responsibility of the policy makers to take rapid action. But they must be given sound advice by the scientists and the thinkers and the religious leaders. We cannot be silent. We must speak out.

The act of speaking out cannot take place if the political and public leadership is not receptive to hearing the message. There must be a dialogue among specialities. There must be a shared responsibility for the commonweal of the planet. It is not enough to issue report after report on the global environment, on development or on poverty. We have developed what I call a 'reporting society' which seems to content itself with the preparation of very accurate, very thoughtful and very helpful reports on subjects of global concern. But we have not yet learned to cross the chasm from reporting to acting.

To cross that chasm we must take into ourselves, into our feelings and our intellects the responsibility to act against the entrenched interests of doing business as usual and to dare to face the risk of acting quickly – in time – even if more information would appear necessary. The scientist, and particularly the health scientist, knows full well that the only total diagnosis that can be performed on a patient can only be done as an autopsy. We must act in time, with the risks that that entails, with the prudence of our human capacity to intuit and to analyse in such a way that we can learn from our mistakes and go forward at a steady or indeed accelerating pace. Only in this way, with a global vision, with foresight and a comprehensive approach, can the new priorities be defined and implemented.

This form of sharing and community building requires that each actor, each person be sovereign unto him or herself. We must begin to look past national boundaries and even regional boundaries to see that our global community is built upon the unique personal capacity and individualities of each person on the planet. It is in releasing these personal sovereignties and these personal potentials that we can arrive at a world energized and dedicated to moving into the 21st century with a utopian but feasible vision of what can be accomplished. No change takes place without passion, without tension. We must not become used to tragedy and catastrophe.

All this, of course, requires freedom. And freedom requires an intense commitment on the part of all political systems to respect the dignity and diversity of all humans in their personal sovereignties, in their cultures and sub-cultures. There is no substitute for freedom and there is no substitute for the defence of freedom by democracy. Only a democratic community, in which all views can be aired and all choices made freely, is capable of supporting a culture of peace. Only respect and responsibility based on the unique sovereignty of each of us can be the basis for a community dedicated to the peaceful and dynamic resolution of problems without resort to violence.

4 Democracy

To that most wise observer and political loser, Alexis de Tocqueville, democracy was only conceivable in the New World in which a new culture was being forged. In his own country, France, during the 1848 'Springtime of peoples', de Tocqueville was steadfast in opposing both Republican and Bonapartist forms of universal male suffrage. Each experiment in democracy (one parliamentary and the other dictatorial) threatened the order and social hierarchy that he saw as the 'juste milieu' between the revolutionary crowd, or mob, and the illiberal excesses of rule by the bayonet.

The revolutionary shocks of the 18th and 19th centuries did, of course, advance the democratic agenda, but they also confirmed many in the belief that order and, indeed reason, were best protected by governance – either formal or informal – by elites of wealth, breeding and leisure. De Tocqueville's unique sensitivity and stubborn commitment to oligarchy, save for North America, seemed, by the 1860s, to be borne out by the loneliness of Abraham Lincoln's struggle for his Union against slaveholders to his south and sceptical elitists or authoritarians across the Atlantic.

In an age of realpolitik and military conflict for the unification of Germany, Italy and the United States of America, only Lincoln could feel the dynamics of a culture of democracy, based on the vast reserves of free and fertile land on the American continent and of a small, still relatively homogeneous population of settlers from the Old Continent. Speaking on the Gettysburg battlefield, that 'dark and bloody ground' where, at last, the Unionists had definitively beaten the Confederate forces, Lincoln could sincerely feel and simply state the issue: 'that government of the people, by the people, and for the people, shall not perish from the earth.'

Yet, within the space of a generation, Lincoln's contemporaries in Europe – Bismarck, Cavour, Jules Ferry, Disraeli and other conservative 'realpolitikers' – had, willy-nilly, begun the construction of democratic political systems in their own countries. The growth of compulsory national primary education systems, of great urban industrial centres, of a cheap mass newspaper press and, above all, of a new sense of national identity drove the democratic process in Europe. An educated workforce was essential to mastering the later, more technical phases of the Industrial Revolution and, remarkably, worker involvement in the political process proved a force for stability and order, a preventive against earlier explosions of desperate, violent protest. The haunting spectre of the barricade was largely dispelled by the ballot and the enormous Socialist or Labour parties of *fin de siècle* Europe showed that orderly democracy could replace the inbuilt instability of formal oligarchy. Marx's own personal affinity for such convinced parliamentary democrats as Edouard Bernstein and Karl Kautsky gives the lie to Lenin's claim that the Bolshevik model was the only 'correct' one. And, in the shambles of the 1917–18 collapse of Germany, Austria–Hungary and Russia, it was the Social Democrats and the Liberals who initially came to the fore. The apogee of the Second International, with Labour ministers in England and strong Socialist and syndicalist movements in the United States and Spain, was soon lost in the struggle among anti-democratic extremisms of the left and right.

The economic crises of the 1920s and 1930s threatened the survival of democratic institutions throughout the industrialized countries. The fragile democracies of Central and Southern Europe were swept away in a maelstrom of nationalism and intolerance. Civil war in Spain, the rise of Fascism, first in Portugal and Italy, and the collapse of the Weimar Republic and its replacement by Nazism set the stage for another war, initially pitting the surviving democracies against Fascist, Nazi and Communist dictatorships. Even American and British democracy seemed threatened by the economic collapse and mass unemployment until the New Deal and the National Government expanded the reach of democratic government into economics, finance and social welfare. Eventually, however, Hitler's invasion of Russia brought Stalin into the United Nations alliance.

From 1848 to 1945, therefore, the fortunes of democracy were anything but consistent. Indeed, mass education, mass culture and mass communications had proved formidable resources for regimes which not only crushed democratic institutions but also sought to extirpate freedom from any aspect of private and public life. 'Democracy' perverted and subverted by mass movements claiming a higher ideological or racial calling seemed to lead naturally and inevitably to totalitarianism. Democracy, however, now given international form in the United Nations Charter and the Universal Declaration of Human Rights, returned to triumph partially in a Europe divided by the cold war. In the Iberian peninsula, authoritarianism survived as 'anti-communism' and, in Eastern Europe, Communist dictatorship replaced defeated

Axis allies in a rim of states around the Soviet border and reached as far as occupied East Germany. Domestically, militarily and in foreign policy, the post-war period saw democracy distorted and often denied in a new global competition of systems and superpowers. Democracies supported dictators as 'bulwarks against communism' while communism, in government or opposition, argued an equally cynical case for 'peoples' democracies'.

As the Third World moved to independence, democracy was rarely the governmental system which prevailed. Military regimes predominated in Latin America and Africa, while Asia's giants divided – India and Japan turning to democracy and China to its own form of communism. In fact, until a decade ago, even democracy's defenders seemed resigned to its minority status in the world and to its survival as a luxury of rich or particularly lucky countries. They had perhaps forgotten that democracy is a very recent invention and that the architects of democracy in North America, Europe and the developing countries were anything but impractical dreamers.

Leaders as different as Lincoln and Disraeli, De Gaulle and Nehru, Adenauer and the democratic reformers of Spain and Portugal, and Raul Alfonsin, Vaclav Havel or Lech Walesa understood that politics is about people and that people cannot work, think, love or grow in the absence of freedom. No genuine community exists, at local or national or, indeed, at international level unless people feel freely and deeply part of it. Coercion or disrespect hurt. The human organism is extremely complex, but it is clear that it is a social, sentient and conscious being from birth to death, capable of imagining the past and transcending the present and projecting into alternative futures. To grow into adulthood, the young need and continually invent new forms of communion among peers, and to grow as adults, 'grown-ups' need communities, large and small, that work together to solve problems, produce and share goods and services and face life's crises with solidarity and dignity.

Democracy is therefore the only political system which cannot be imposed from the top or the centre because its culture only grows from the bottom up, from neighbourhoods and villages – the grass roots where people live and work. It is also the only political system that celebrates its own vulnerability to disruption, intolerance, mass hysteria, confusion, paralysis and even collapse. A lack of prior restraint on things said, done or even conspired is vital to democracy and also potentially fatal. Those in power are required to limit their personal ambition, disclose their scandals and errors, welcome hostile enquiry and questions and accept defeat by stepping down. Opposition is not merely tolerated, it is encouraged, often by public facilities and government funds.

All the risks inherent in a context of freedom are freely accepted because 'democrats', of the right, centre or left, know that democracy is also the only political system that has the ethical and moral force to be reborn when smothered and to gestate in even the most hostile of environments. It is a continuously evolving dialogue between the uniqueness of each individual and the search for community, between freedom and responsibility, between orderly disorder and disorderly order. Democracy *is* a culture because it is, above all, an attitude of self and society, an aesthetic and an ideal about 'good behaviour' and 'character'. A true secular religion, democracy prefers doubt to blind faith and pragmatism to dogma. It is intensely private and public simultaneously because it is a way of life that, ideally, permeates our attitudes to others in the intimacy of our local communities and in the panoply of national symbols of legitimate authority.

Born in slave-holding societies (ancient Athens and Jefferson's America), democracy requires leisure, education and reflection, since it involves an endless series of choices and decisions. It relishes the style of egalitarianism, but applauds the leader who moves ahead of the pack. It respects the law, detests arbitrary authority and admires the judges, jurors or legislators who ignore, reject or change outdated rules. Most of all, democracy is to do with words – spoken, written and rhythmic – with the poetry of power at chronic risk and subject to permanent public examination.

As ancient Athens showed us, and Shakespeare and Machiavelli more than broadly hinted, democracy is theatre, a perpetual play of words and gestures carrying thoughts and emotions between leaders and their constituents. And the audience names the cast. Bertrand Russell in his 1948–9 Reith Lectures recognized that Athenian democracy was seriously flawed by the exclusion of women and by slavery, but he argued:

> Every citizen could vote on every issue, he did not have to delegate his power to a representative. He could elect executive officers, including generals and could get them condemned if they displeased a majority. The number of citizens was small enough for each man to feel that he counted ... In the one respect of allowing for individual initiative it was greatly superior to anything that exists in the modern world.

The problem – as Russell and others saw it very clearly by the middle of the present century – was that if the democratic theatre of Athens was a small and community-bounded institution integrated into everyday life, and if Shakespeare's Globe was a similar kind of theatre moving towards the democratic revolutions of the 17th and 18th centuries, then the world that they had built is much bigger and perhaps too big to encompass a full personal participation of citizens in democracy. Jefferson himself, in the next rebirth of democracy, based very much on the classical readings of Greek and Latin antiquity, lived in the bounded world of a small planter aristocracy in the state of Virginia and interacted directly on a face-to-face basis with his fellow Enlightenment thinkers. Madison was his neighbour. Hamilton, his great rival, was a fellow member of the Cabinet and, for a while, a close friend. All the authors of the American Constitution and the Declaration of Independence knew each other by correspondence and by face-to-face contact in a very small world.

That world encompassed many different ways of organizing political and cultural life. Virginia was a slave state, while the New England culture of Massachusetts, home of Sam Adams and the future President John Adams, was a stronghold of free labour and puritanism. Yet, alone on the continent, cut off from Europe, far from London, they continued the Enlightenment in their own way: as an intimate and direct grouping of yeoman farmers. Jefferson's notion of democracy was firmly based on the availability of land and on the capacity of each individual immigrant to the New World to acquire land and become a farmer. Alexander Hamilton was more sceptical of democracy, but, as a key author of the Constitution, he propounded a more urban and industrial view of the future of the New World. The Constitution of the United States is a far more conservative document than Jefferson's Declaration of Independence and seeks to circumscribe government and popular participation as much as possible. Yet, in the first generation of the new republic, it was Jefferson and, later, Jackson and Lincoln who would prevail and democracy would take on a more Jeffersonian content.

The point, however, is that this debate about the nature of North American democracy took place within a very small and familiar set of political actors. The Lincoln–Douglas debates which took place across Illinois and throughout the north, prior to Lincoln's presidential nomination, was a theatre performed before thousands. And yet Lincoln and Douglas – opposed on the question of the abolition of slavery – had both been the suitors of the woman who became Mary Todd Lincoln. Lincoln had indeed grown up not more than 20 miles from the birthplace of Jefferson Davis, who became the President of the Confederacy. Thus the initial vision of democracy was one of a small, communicating, permanently interacting group of individuals, leaders and followers in constant contact and dialogue with each other.

By our own time, Bertrand Russell would be one of a number of thinkers, including Sir Isaiah Berlin and many political scientists and philosophers in democratic societies who were coming to an awareness of the danger of *bigness* in democratic systems. They had seen through the great depression and the crisis of war, the expansion of government into areas that had never before been subjected to public control, particularly those areas concerned with economics, finance and social welfare which have generated the development of vast bureaucracies responsible to democratic authority. In this necessary expansion of the governmental system in these democracies, the sense of community, the sense of personal involvement in the democratic process, was felt to have been lost in the development of barriers between the governed and the leaders. Radio and, later, television could give the feeling of being communicated with among the governed but at the same time ended a kind of continual process of direct involvement with the candidate or with the leader. Within the bureaucracy, the decisions of the leaders were now carried out by unelected, appointed civil servants operating within sets of impersonal rules and procedures.

Max Weber, of whom we have spoken before, saw this conflict as that between what he called *Gemeinschaft*, or community, and *Gesellschaft*, or corporate organization or bureaucracy. As Russell put it:

> Among the things which are in danger of being unnecessarily sacrificed to democratic equality, perhaps the most important is self-respect. ... If a man has not this quality, he will feel that majority opinion, or governmental opinion, is to be treated as infallible, and such a way of feeling, if it is general, makes both moral and intellectual progress impossible.

He went on to say that 'A democratic regime ... *can* give complete opportunity for the preservation of self-respect. But it *may* do quite the opposite'.

In other words, the distance of the individual or the small, local community from the levers of power or from interaction with the leadership can create a situation which Weber called *alienation* and Durkheim called *anomie*, in which the individual's commitment to the democratic culture atrophies, in which the sense of having initiative and responsibility for keeping the process alive can die. This is not merely a theoretical question. After all, it was the seeming impersonality of the Weimar democracy that gave way to the intense and emotional search for a racial community that was the underpinning of the Nazi regime. Similarly, the frustration of Italian youth with the slow workings of Italian democracy after the First World War had much to do with the political career of Benito Mussolini as he shifted from being a leading socialist to becoming the leader of the Fascist movement. Democracy is a vulnerable system and it is particularly vulnerable when those who should be committed to it, those who should be concerned about its survival, are demobilized by a sense of exclusion. In such circumstances, the politics of a community, of individual respect and tolerance among people, becomes the politics of rage, prejudice and violence.

The problem of 'bigness' or, more appropriately, the question of distance from the individual and the local to the central government or to the leadership is one which remains a conundrum for democrats everywhere. As democracy now experiences a rebirth in Eastern Europe, Asia, Latin America and Africa, is it not a fundamental question to be confronted? We currently enjoy a technology and a capacity for linking individuals to the political system more closely and more continuously than ever before, but we have not yet harnessed this force of information and dialogue to the democratic system. The computer, the television and the interactive media provide a way in which democracy can almost achieve or reachieve its Athenian or Jeffersonian quality.

As a participant in the transition of my own country from authoritarianism to democracy, I personally experienced the difficulty of making democracy a living reality to the people of my region. On an electoral trip to a small rural village I met an elderly farmer who was eloquent on the subject, and troubling as well. I had made a brief presentation to my supporters concerning the transition Spanish society was going through on the political and many other levels, when the farmer took me aside. He said, 'Professor Mayor, I wake up in the morning and I put my farm equipment on the mule. I lead the mule out to the fields and I work from dawn till dusk in my fields and as the sun goes down I come home. This is my life ['como toda la vida de Dios'] and I feel that the democracy of which you speak is way over there in Madrid because my life is exactly the way it has always been.' On another, equally instructive level, many of my students at the university felt that Granada was so far from Madrid that the lofty ideas they were studying, the passionate commitments they felt, could not really be put into effect at the local level. When I launched the campaign for the prevention of mental retardation, working with pregnant women and treating the newborn, I met with initial resistance in many institutions, including the university and even some of the students. They held the strong belief that problems were solved from the centre, from Madrid. Yet, if it is difficult to mobilize an elite of scholars, how much more difficult is it to create an informed and active citizenry among the 'men and women in the street'.

On still another, more global level, we have seen in recent years a continual series of very important and very interesting reports prepared by panels headed by Willy Brandt, or by Prime Minister Gro Harlem Brundtland of Norway, or by Julius Nyerere of Tanzania. All these reports are very useful and important. But I must add that they help to create the 'reporting society', in which questions of environment and development and the shape of the future global community frequently take the form of a very small minority speaking only to itself. The question, therefore, is how to revitalize democracy toward direct involvement of citizens of all backgrounds in the feeling and the reality of having a role to play in the future of their locality, their region and of the planet as a whole. As Bertrand Russell put it, 'As a result of mere size, government becomes increasingly remote from the governed and tends, even in a democracy, to have an independent life of its own.' The problem is that, even in the most deeply rooted democracies, in those with the greatest technological and economic capacities for democratic participation to take place, the government and the leadership seem more and more distant from those living everyday lives in local situations. Moreover, those living these everyday lives, whether they are intellectuals at the university or farmers in villages, have a sense of impotence and of not being able to work on the major problems of the day. Democratic politics seem more and more to have become the specialized business of a very small, professional minority of politicians, experts and civil servants.

Democracy loses its feeling and its cultural consistency when leaders no longer lead and followers no longer actively support public affairs. The distance of leader from follower, of follower from fellow citizen, caused by the complexity and distance of modern democratic systems, can only be confronted as a problem of education, of culture and of communication. The questions dealt with on the political level seem more and more complicated and, indeed, heavily scientific, particularly as we confront problems of the environment and of our impact on the ecosystem that gives us life. Somehow we in the scientific community, the political community, the educational community, or the cultural community, have not been able to bond our interests and our capacities in communication and education with the civic culture of democracy. For democracy is an active thing. It requires, particularly in matters of environment and development, many acts and gestures by private citizens, much feeling and commitment in order to carry through the very profound changes that we will have to pursue in establishing a better equilibrium with nature and a better equilibrium between the wealthy countries and the poor.

The irony of our situation, here at the end of the 20th century, is perhaps best represented when we think that we recently celebrated the 200th anniversary of the publication of the *Rights of Man*, by Jefferson' s friend and Washington' s propagandist, Thomas Paine. Paine wrote, on the subject of democracy, perhaps one of the most important paragraphs to justify the equality of citizens and their involvement in decision making:

> Every age and generation must be as free to act for itself in all cases as the ages and generations which preceded it. The vanity and presumption of governing beyond the grave is the most ridiculous and insolent of all tyrannies. Man has no property in man, neither has any generation a property in the generations which are to follow.

He was arguing that only by direct participation of equal citizens could new solutions be given to old and new problems. He felt that government was not a technical and difficult thing; that government was a matter of continual action by all concerned. The inventor of the term 'United States of America', Jefferson's friend in helping to write the Declaration of Independence and the author of *Common Sense* – the pamphlet that raised the morale of the American revolutionary forces – Tom Paine felt, with the strength of his Quaker convictions, that rule by the few was an enemy of our freedom to move through history towards a future of understanding and community. He wrote: 'A body of men holding themselves accountable to nobody, ought not to be trusted by anybody.'

In a brilliant bicentenary article on Tom Paine, Michael Foot, the former Labour leader, points out that Paine was very much influenced by Jonathan Swift's humour and by his profound democratic convictions. As Foot writes, '"Government", says Swift, "is a plain thing and fitted to the capacity of many heads".' Yet this doctrine of popular participation in government resulted in the *Rights of Man* being one of the most banned publications in English history. Thomas Erskine, who was to be the future Lord Chancellor, strongly defended Paine and the Rights of Man. As quoted by Foot, Erskine's defence remains one of the most important legal descriptions of democratic governance. He argued:

> Let reason be opposed to reason and argument to argument and every good government will be safe. Opinions and understanding are not such wares as to be monopolized and traded in by tickets, statutes and standards. We must not think to make a staple commodity of all the knowledge in the land, to mark and license it like our broadcloth and our woolpacks ... the stage, my lords, and the press, are two of our out-sentries and if we remove them, if we hoodwink them, if we throw them in fetters, this enemy will surprise us.

Knowledge, reason, the stage, and the press – these in one paragraph are a summation of the culture of democracy in its institutional and legal forms. If Erskine lost his case, he none the less had laid the foundations for the advent of democracy in the future. Paine left London in 1792 for Paris, where he was to become a well-regarded figure and even an elected member of the French National Assembly. He was horrified by the Terror and was imprisoned by it, only to escape and die, poor and forgotten, back in his adopted America. Yet the importance of Paine in understanding the culture of democracy remains central, and still retains its pre-eminence. If democracy is the true creed of the modern world, it was Paine's *Rights of Man* that was the Bible of the new secular religion. Paine abhorred any notion of establishing a new authority or a new creed. He constantly insisted that all ideas, including his own, must be subjected to free debate and above all free printing: the power of the printed word which had made the revolutions of his own age.

The cultural roots of democracy and its own culture as a political system draw extensively on a history which is both classical and religious. From Herodotus describing the politics of Athens to Thucydides describing the conflict between democratic Athens and totalitarian Sparta and through to Plutarch, images of democracy and of a kind of austere participatory rectitude have come down to us across the millennia. Democracy continues through such profound symbolisms and beliefs as Jesus telling the disciples to preach to 'publicans and sinners'. It continues in the sense of John Bull's perfect aphorism from the great English peasant uprisings of the 14th century: 'When Adam delved and Eve span who was then the gentleman?' It is further borne out historically and symbolically in the next century by a peasant girl leading the chivalry of France.

These are active notions of the democracy of our souls, and during the German peasants' revolt of 1525, the leaders of the serfs, urging the abolition of serfdom, argued with Martin Luther that 'Christ redeemed us all with his precious blood, the shepherd as well as the noble, the lowest as well as the highest, none being excepted.' Indeed, one of the most basic debates about democracy took place within Cromwell's victorious 'army of the saints' at Putney, where it was argued similarly that God had invested all with souls and with the possibility of grace and that all should directly participate in the political process.

In the Iberian peninsula, the enduring power of charters, traditions and privileges dating back to the medieval guilds acted as a brake on arbitrariness and despotism. The tacit alliance of monarchy and commoners (those with no privileges), as opposed to feudal abuse and the ambitions of both clergy and nobility, is a recurring theme in classical Spanish theatre, as in Lope (*Peribáñez and the Commander of Ocaña, Fuenteovejuna*), and Calderón (*The Mayor of Zalamea*). Among the most important theoretical antecedents, we must give pride of place to Fray Bartolomé de las Casas who brilliantly defended the rights of the natives in Latin America – in the 16th century! Later on, Luis Vives and Francisco de Vitoria both contributed to the conceptual framework of equality and freedom, essential components of the rights of man, but without doubt, it was Padre Suárez, in negating the theory of the divine right of royalty and defending the thesis of popular sovereignty, who established the highest and most avant-garde points of reference, thus influencing Descartes and Leibnitz and all European philosophy of the 17th and 18th centuries.

The breach that started opening at the beginning of the 19th century, because of the War of Independence against the Napoleonic forces, made way for liberalism and democracy for the ordinary Spanish people. In 1812, the Cadiz Constitution laid the foundations of national sovereignty and representation of the people through suffrage. It abolished the privileges of the nobility and put an end to the Inquisition. As many historians have attested, it was the most advanced document of its time. Although it incorporated many English and French ideas, it was also an effort to unite the rights and liberties proclaimed by liberalism, with the traditions and principles of age-old Hispanic heritage. At the same time, in Latin America, Bolívar, San Martín and Hidalgo blew to pieces an empire which had lasted three centuries and, in the name of liberty and in extremely precarious circumstances, founded a constellation of new republics.

In Latin America, the democratic and constitutional ideal was to experience many setbacks over the coming decades. But it was so firmly rooted that any tyranny was obliged to call on the defence of freedom as an alibi or to proclaim a new constitution. This is, no doubt, the tribute that vice pays to virtue. But the courage and self-denial of those founders have remained a high point of historical reference for the rebirth of democracy Latin America is experiencing at the end of the 20th century.

The equality of souls and perfectibility of humanity in its quest for spiritual salvation lie at the heart of all the world's great religions and constitute one of the most powerful foundations for democracy in all cultures. Mahatma Gandhi, synthesizing all of India's religious traditions, preached in his non-violent stance an approach to democracy which resonated with profound values. Gandhi's example of suffering, humility, simplicity, and leading by serving and teaching, is an example of democratic leadership which sets India apart from many of the countries of the developing world. Yet wherever democracy exists, or where it is muzzled or suppressed, the fundamental democratic, political act is always that of leadership. And that leadership always involves the question of dialogue with ordinary people and the capacity to learn and to teach. A culture of democracy is therefore ultimately a culture of education and continual growth.

The failure of democratic leadership, for which we all share some responsibility, has been the loss of this passion for education and learning in the political sector. Somehow, our specialization has set politics apart from other areas of the pursuit of knowledge and the pursuit of a sense of understanding and working on problems. Should the very numerous younger generation of many of the Third-World countries and the very important, if smaller, younger generation of the industrialized countries lose their sense of involvement in community affairs and feel themselves marginalized from a routinized world in which they have little say, then the future of democracy is at risk. And that risk would result largely from the loss of a culture of democracy in which democratic institutions and democratic conduct can take root and flourish.

Those who have made enormous financial gains within a less than democratic system and see everything in terms of cost–benefit or short-term profit cannot understand what democracy really means. They are trying to avoid transition to a truly democratic regime which would put their own privileges in jeopardy. It is not the affluent minority, submerged in superfluous commodities, who can guide the world, in these moments of hope, towards freedom. I know that it will not be easy to overcome the immense interests opposing change, but we are not here in the UN system to be managers of institutions. We are here to be tireless promoters of change. The present mood will be difficult to reverse. Nevertheless, it is clear that if we fail to reduce disparities and assymetries – starting with the greatest, of 20 per cent of the world's population enjoying 80 per cent of the available resources – those of us in positions of high responsibility will be judged very severely by future generations. Because now change *is feasible*. We have the ways and means – if we are able to alter our priorities and habits. It is purely a question of *political will*.

I hope that one day, perhaps not too far away, the UN system will be able to face all challenges to global security, and the 'green helmets' will join the blue ones in their peace function. Democracy is, I believe, the answer because only freedom provides the context in which we can seek new knowledge and new solutions to problems. Only freedom permits us to transcend prejudice or ignorance and move forward to new ways of approaching our existence as individuals, as communities and as a world.

How much poverty and ignorance can the wings of freedom support? That was the question for Dante Caputo, President of the 1989 UN General Assembly. Democracy means sharing; it means participation. In short, it means *to count* as a citizen and not merely to be taken into account. The great Spanish philosopher Miguel de Unamuno reminded us in Valencia, at the beginning of the 20th century, that only those who are educated are free, and they are freer when better cultivated. All democracies built on ignorance are fragile and vulnerable. 'Culture means security,' wrote Ortega y Gasset, 'and only a solid foundation allows for further achievements.'

Democracy cannot be installed by decree or as a requisite for negotiations or loans. It is an attitude that is forged every day from early childhood through to old age. The pedagogy of democracy is the pedagogy of peace. It is a process having many teachers and schools – parents and relatives, friends and educators, media, textbooks, advertisements, publicity, authorities, and particularly local authorities, since it is at the municipal level that democracy, 'direct' democracy, reaches its peak, where citizenship is more real. This is why I often dream of a 'municipal' UNESCO, of the defences of peace being built 'down-town' in towns and cities and, at the same time, in the minds of every man and woman throughout the world.

5 The Democratic Dynamics of Culture and the Culture of Democracy

Culture is the overarching set of symbols, aesthetics and significations which weave our lives together as something purposeful and meaningful from birth to death. This is not only with a sense of our own individual lives and our identity but the way in which our communities knit themselves together and express themselves as groups sharing concerns and experiences in ways that work to project memories and discoveries and even traumas and fears across the boundaries of our mortal existence to future generations. They are the ways in which we amuse ourselves, give dimension to our lives and transcend the daily and mundane in order to seek a higher level of existence and importance in our lives. In an old-fashioned sense, culture, or what we call high culture, was the affair of very few people lucky enough or privileged enough to create music, prose, poetry or the plastic arts in a way which others – also the 'happy few' – could then enjoy. Thus culture is, above all, everyday behaviour: behaviour that reflects everyone's values; one's thoughts and ideas, the personal choice made between distinct options, each person's unique answer to essential questions, the outcome in each one of us of acquired knowledge, the stamp imprinted on us by our social environment.

In this sense, culture has a personal as well as a global dimension. Beliefs, religions, ideologies and fashions are matters of choice by communities: by many individuals coming together and sharing certain sensibilities. These are not necessarily spontaneous events in the cultural history of a given society. Rather, they involve conflict between different sensitivities, conflict with previous cultural habits that give way to new experiments in feeling, and new forms of creativity and aesthetics.

51

The force of culture, and of change in culture, is its profound impact on our feelings and its value-laden quality. All culture carries with it a summons to reflect on our ethical responsibilities and also on our central responsibilities to ourselves, which are to feel, to open ourselves to the world around us and to accept new responsibilities. New feelings are often irritating, often troubling but they make us grow and develop in different ways.

Thus, perhaps, in a cultural–political sense, the most deep-running events are those which we may not fully consider cultural revolutions but which indeed were and are. In ages which had no institutional experience of democracy as a political form, the ability of Galileo to say *sotto voce* 'Eppur si muove' when the Church insisted that the sun revolves around the Earth, or of Joan of Arc to stand at the stake preparing to die while refusing to abjure her personal image of a deeply individual God presaged broader struggles for free enquiry, tolerance and equality. These were events that challenged institutions and were far more profound and long-term than a mere political event. They carry the force of a personality and of a culture – in other words a set of values – which were so strong and so deeply held that they could stand up to the 'Establishment' of their day.

Science is the result of a democratic culture based on respect for the individual's capacity to enquire and find new explanations for old facts, or better explanations involving new facts. Free enquiry and the scientific and technological revolution of our age are fundamentally based on democratic and libertarian principles of the freedom of individuals and teams of researchers to pose problems and find their solutions without any 'prejudice' or prior restraint on the findings which they may discover. Similarly, the novel and poetry are based on concepts of individual growth and development and the freedom to change and use language in new rhythms and new ways which are a tribute to a tolerance of individual difference. In the same way, music and art are forms which call upon the audience to experience often shocking and troubling images or sets of sounds which stretch our senses and force our feelings and our minds to open to a large variety of patterns.

All of this is a form of learning and involves the willingness on the part of the community to accept challenges and influences which are not expected. These are highly temporal and secular questions involving the way we define ourselves and our capacity to accept that time is not frozen. Maturity means being open to all interaction and defending our identity in the name of cultural diversity as a source of enrichment. Some 2500 years ago, Heraclitus taught us that nobody bathes twice in the same river. Our surrounding, natural and man-made context is always in flux and we must adapt and move with these changes as individuals and as communities in ways which create a better and more meaningful life for ourselves and those who will live beyond our own deaths.

This involves a set of – for want of a better word – contracts between ourselves and our neighbours, between ourselves and our children which emphasize tolerance and mutual respect and even a capacity to open ourselves beyond our existing limits to ensure growth, not merely individual growth, although that is fundamentally important, especially in the cultural context, but, more importantly, community growth. Within the community new ideas, new sensibilities and new ways of acting, dressing or communicating are constantly in motion and constantly worthy of our tolerance in an effort to foster mutual benefit as well as to avoid uniformity. Quite rightly, many people are afraid of biological cloning, without realizing that cultural cloning is already happening, although in a rather more subtle way.

The plurality of cultures, this conflict of aesthetics and of ways of feeling, is in fact a way of promoting freedom. Because it offers us a wide range of choices, choices often not easy to make, it forces us to accept the responsibility for the texture of our lives. The workplace is also a cultural institution and, as it evolves more and more under the impact of computers and other technological changes, it too reflects a higher and higher sense of freeing the human being from the old rhythms of the assembly line and moving towards levels of leisure and creativity unknown to our parents' generation. However, this freedom we have become used to may turn into passivity and intellectual isolation if our daily work gradually becomes implanted by 'externalization' through audiovisual media and computer games and so on which are replacing thought, individual opinions, and social gatherings. Individuality is succumbing to outside forces: 'cultural products' developed by different institutions are taking over a dangerously large part of the self. Therefore we must use the tools science and technology put at our disposal, and not let ourselves be used by them.

All of these changes in culture involve a constant process of learning and teaching. To take two modern examples of the breakdown of old-fashioned barriers between so-called 'high' and 'low' cultures, we should consider the impact of jazz in the world of music and that of television in the world of all the performing arts. Jazz certainly did not begin as something conceived of as high culture. Nor did it originate from European sensibilities or art forms. Yet jazz and its African and Latin American rhythms have come to occupy a position of privileged freedom in innovation and in the exploration of new rhythms and sounds unknown to classical music. Indeed, we have arrived at a point where jazz and classical music and jazz and popular music (in the form of rock and roll and rhythm and blues) have fused and become syntheses beyond any pre-existing schools of musical creation.

Television has brought the world of elite and popular culture directly into the homes of millions of people who would never have had access to the theatre, the concert hall or, for that matter, the newsroom. Marshall McLuhan, describing the importance of the global village, touched on the whole issue of very numerous different forms of cultural expression becoming directly available to audiences in the most remarkable and sudden sense. The real kind of power of television to broadcast both an image and a sound into the home, describing current events or introducing new forms of music and dance or theatre is particularly relevant to our lives, because television with its force and its acuity can spark changes in the way we organize our perceptions and, perhaps best of all, it has opened us to a sense that what we experience in our daily lives may not be everything there is we need to know.

Of course, the commercial aspects of television or popular music, or even certain forms of mass-circulation literature, have their less attractive or challenging sides. Aimed at as big an audience as possible, they may not often rise to the level of expectation many of us have of cultural production. The answer to this, of course, is that, as education spreads more fully through societies and as people's expectations of leisure increase, the demands for better cultural production and for more sincere and challenging artistic content will evolve. This is certainly the case in the more wealthy societies, where the electronic media, particularly television, previously dominated by a few large networks, have given way to extremely profitable and interesting 'micro-markets' that meet the cultural needs of a wide variety of ethnic, linguistic, social and professional groups in highly varied societies. Thus the pluralism of culture ultimately seems to prevail.

However, a world divided between a minority living in relative affluence and a vast global majority living very close to the poverty line requires a vision of culture which goes beyond the local or even the national. Sharing the global commons requires not only an environmental sensitivity but also a concern for social justice. In the wealthier countries, the outpouring of concern and of real support to victims of environmental and other forms of tragedy such as famine in the Third World is an example of the way in which the new access to immediate information can break down the barriers of space and perhaps of prejudice or ignorance and bind the world more closely together.

The global village faces three challenges central to democracy and culture: population growth rates, migration to big cities ('rural drain') and peaceful inter-ethnic coexistence. Education, particularly of young women, is the best way to reduce population growth. In a variety of cultural and religious settings, birth rates have declined radically with increased access to formal or non-formal education for women and girls. Rural emigration can be moderated by an imaginative set of actions: incentives for development of micro-industries in the countryside;

army transport assistance for peacetime health emergencies; investment in rural educational centres of excellence; an increase in the percentage of the gross domestic product devoted to agricultural and agroindustrial R&D; and so on. There is no democracy if intercultural dialogue is not assured. It is essential to generate behavioural attitudes at an early stage: to know the other is the best preventive strategy. The culture of democracy and the democracy of culture come together around the concept of education, particularly around the related phenomenon of leadership. Those who led the great mass movement for popular participation in politics and those who created the movements for independence in the Third World were all great teachers. They were not propounding certainties and unquestioned orders to the people they mobilized. They sought, with a certain degree of humility and strength, to persuade and to involve vast numbers of individuals in actions they had never previously even imagined. Gandhi's capacity to speak to so many different religious and linguistic groups, Cromwell's capacity to organize an army based on democratic practices in a society which had never practised democracy, Jefferson's ability in a slave-holding society to criticize slavery and propound democracy are all examples of a humble, yet iron-willed ability to teach. The capacity to teach and to learn, to speak and to hear, to put forward ideas and to alter them or to adapt them to people's needs involves love.

Democratic leadership is not in any sense weak. It is strong in its capacity to accept criticism, to listen, to bargain, to change, to keep fundamentals. The great leaders of democratic movements have always been those most sensitive to the cultural milieu around them and to the power of words to touch people. Their love, their openness to the suffering and needs of others, has usually been expressed in a leadership which is strong, strong in its capacity to enter into a dialogue and to be open to change.

Balanced finely between the meaningfulness and symbolism of the past and the requirements of the present, the leadership of democratic movements or of democracies at points of crisis has always shown an ability to bring people forward from a past which may have been characterized by prejudice or a sense of limits towards new goals and a sense of community. It is in this capacity to weld a community out of disparate groups and individuals that democracy's best leaders have shown their greatest talent. That has always been present in an ability to speak carefully and clearly and to act on what was spoken and what was learned in a way which built the confidence of people in their own ability to contribute to the community's progress.

The most remarkable features of democracy are its relatively short-lived career in many societies and its capacity to grow. After all, until a generation ago democracy excluded women. Yet eventually, and perhaps with a great deal of hesitancy, this essential half of the human race was not only involved in the democratic process of the vote but ultimately moved to positions of leadership. Thus the earlier anti-democratic prejudices that said that women could not fully participate in the political process ultimately fell before an ethical commitment to involve all elements of the community in political decisions. The idea of women not being allowed to participate fully in the political process has gradually made way, with some notorious exceptions, even in countries of the purest 'democratic' tradition, for the ethical compromise of involving all community members in the decision-making process. The same holds true for the belated abolition of slavery and the practice of earlier generations in excluding the poor or certain ethnic minorities in their societies from full, democratic participation.

What this means is that democracy is a dynamic of expanding the community, of accepting its different features as an act of encompassing rather than excluding. Because democracy is a community developing its decision-making capacities through time, it can change and it can grow. Because of this, we must consider what we can do in the present situation, in the world and in our local communities, to make democracy an active rather than a passive phenomenon. As the educational world has moved from a sense of simply laying out a set of truths that children or young people must learn to a more direct and heuristic experiential learning, so, indeed, must the political community move to a greater sense of direct involvement of the citizen in the problems of the day. As Jorge Guillen says in one of his best known poems: 'Man is tired of being a thing…'. Let me say again, democracy is not counting people; democracy is when people count.

Each citizen must matter: this will be the final stage in guiding the education strategy of leaders, with their political ('pol-ethical') role of decision making. It is the nexus of the local with the global. Despite the difficulties this will entail, this seems to be the most effective way of countering the social and environmental global crisis we are facing today, which has come about largely through the increasing poverty of so many. If, from a very early age, we learn ethical, political and scientific notions, we can develop the capacity to assume responsibility in working on solutions to these challenges, whether local, national or global. Everything depends – but how often we forget it! – on learning to care for others.

It is the role of leadership, institutional or personal, in its best form to overcome the sense of paralysis or helplessness. Leadership as teaching, as a servant to the growth of our minds and our capacities, is a summons to our own ability to lead ourselves. The great leaders have always produced more leadership around them. All too often, high achievements are not copied. Power is wielded alone, with solitude as company. The surrounding passivity jeopardizes the leader's efforts and vision. The great leaders have always welcomed debate and conflict: conflict of ideas, conflict of solutions, conflict of approaches. This is the greatest strength of democracy. It is its tolerance, and even enjoyment, of different choices and different ways of saying things, of different meanings for different phrases. It is the continual expansion of what was the participation of a small elite in the decisions that shape all our lives to making all of us members of the elite that shapes the life of the planet. The creative irony, but certainly not the contra-diction, of this democratic tolerance, of difference and disagreement is that it builds peace. By channelling and respecting many different views and sensibilities, democracy removes many of the bases for violence and permits us to think about the price of peace. That price is considerable, but I am convinced that it can be paid and paid generously when all are involved in the decisions needed for building peace.

Change will not come about if there is no tension, or no daily, permanent concessions, no bold action taken on clear, precise ideals. What a great mistake has been made – and still is being made – in trying to export 'democratic models' instead of sharing and teaching the universal principles of liberty, justice and care for others. These are the foundations on which the democracy can be built the world over. Today's world must be made to see the irrelevance of its classes and privileges. We should remember Leonardo da Vinci's maxim: 'When a boat is sinking, all the passengers are in equal danger.' All of us, irre-spective of colour, age, sex, race, class or beliefs, are in the same boat. Warned of his common fate, no-one will hide how much he knows or how much he has. In order to keep the boat afloat and reach safe harbour, all aboard will give their all. That all the passengers should be equal is the fundamental requisite of universal democracy.

6 The Price of Peace

> They shall beat their swords into ploughshares, and their spears into pruninghooks: nation shall not lift up sword against nation, neither shall they learn war any more.   (Isaiah 2.4.)

We must have the strength to recognize that the outcome of the warring civilization is not, if it is to be considered in its entirety, satisfactory, nor does it measure up to human dignity. We measure the strength of a country by its soldiers, by its tanks and fighter-bombers, and not by its medical centres for the study of tumours, or biomedical research, or by the number of teachers, doctors and nurses. Throughout the centuries, the only language that has been understood is that of weapons. The destructive force that has been reached is so immense, that, in 1988, the two superpowers recognized, at a truly historic moment, that a confrontation could mean mutual annihilation.

The winds of freedom began to blow across all latitudes and the effects of *perestroika* reached their zenith when the Berlin wall and the iron curtain tumbled with unforeseen rapidity, showing that no ideology can progress when it is imposed. This was the triumph of democracy, of public freedom, of the free expression of thought of all citizens. It must be stated, however, that, instead of interpreting this as the victory of certain principles and values, there were more than a few observers who reduced this great event to simple economic terms. Those who had struggled for years, dreaming of finding at the end of the long, dark tunnel, the outstretched hands of those who had shared the same ideals, were greeted by bankers, brokers and corporate lawyers and salesmen. Business is, of course, important, but democratic ideals need respect.

We find ourselves living at a time of great possibilities. There are many transformations which, progressively, will have to be introduced into our habits, customs and strategies on the national as well as international scale so that the first page of a new culture of peace can begin to be written. For that to happen, we must accept the complexity of the questions, the globality both of the problems and of their solutions and

59

emerging international challenges. Then, as experts with all the details of what war costs, we must then begin to calculate the price of peace. We know that it will be no easy task and that there are enormous public and private interests committed to defending the culture of war.

Above all, it must be recognized that there are limits to political decision-making capacities. Now it is not merely a question of short-term economic analyses but of the scientific and technical aspects as well. We now need diagnoses which allow for the adoption of measures before irreversible situations are reached. Interaction and interdependence with other countries must be kept in mind. The prosperity and security of a particular country will no longer depend solely on its own development and on its friendly relations with neighbouring countries, but on the reduction, on a global scale, of the inequalities and injustice that endanger the whole of humanity. First and foremost, we must strive to produce and share knowledge. In an information age, knowledge – without doubt – is the real wealth and power of nations.

Excessive demographic growth, precisely where poverty is greatest; changes in the environment; violence and intolerance brought about particularly by injustice, lack of equality and ignorance – these are the challenges that will progressively persuade those in command, those who hold positions of responsibility in the public and private sectors, that everything can no longer be seen in purely economic terms. Ecological, social and moral concerns deserve priority. All these transformations should be realized at an extraordinarily accelerated pace. For decades, while the status quo of the cold war prevailed, institutions and instruments of international cooperation could make only limited, though valuable, contributions to solving questions of peace, security and development. Now, however, everything must be rethought. The role of the UN in its peace-keeping capacity is unprecedented. At the same time, it is asked to intervene in matters of energy, environment, drug trafficking and arms dealing. By constantly asking for help in peace-keeping we run the risk of forgetting the primary function, which is to avoid war and promote social and economic development. The most visible, (and the most costly) section of the United Nations system is still its armed forces. We have the necessary funds in our budgets for armies, but we have not enough to fight poverty and desperation – the root of all disorder and tension which degenerate into war. Perhaps at no other point in recent history has the conceptual and practical evolution of the international system been so great, both in quality and tempo. It is imperative that we adapt in order to establish new ways for the future.

A study group, chaired by Swedish Prime Minister Carlsson[1], estimated that, in the north, in the year 2000, peace dividends could reach some 200 or 300 billion dollars. They believe that in several industrialized countries the greater part of such peace dividends must be used in human development (education and health especially) as well as for environmental protection. Between 30 and 40 billion dollars of the peace dividend should be earmarked each year for international cooperation, they suggest. In the south, the peace dividend should come in large part from the developing countries' own efforts, especially those countries that today waste between 200 and 300 billion dollars a year on arms. In many countries the military budget is two to three times that invested in education and health. A large part of what is spent today on the armed forces should be invested in human development, meaning that the countries' leaders must resist the enormous pressures they are under to buy arms.

UNICEF (United Nations Children's Fund) reckons that in order to avoid infant mortality and undernutrition or malnutrition for 50 million children, 2.5 billion dollars are needed each year. With 1 billion dollars a year, the World Health Organization (WHO)'s 'Health For All' programme could be put into effect. Finally, according to the calculations of UNESCO and the United Nations Development Programme (UNDP), 5 billion dollars a year would enable all children to have access to primary school education by the year 2000. These outlays are part of the price of peace.

Although in the 1980s there was a clear slowing of progress in the developing countries, and most specifically in the least developed countries, from a broader perspective it is evident that efforts made both nationally and internationally, efforts to improve the quality of life, have achieved important advances. In 1960, life expectancy in Third-World countries was 46, while in 1987 it was 62; in 1970, the number of literate people was 43 per cent of the adult population, while in 1985 the figures reached 60 per cent. Poverty should be eradicated in 25 years. For this to happen, between now and the year 2000, the following goals must be reached: primary education for all children; equal attendance of boys and girls in schools; and a one-third reduction of the infant mortality rate. While encouraging primary education, developing countries must not forget training technicians and creating or maintaining a nucleus – however modest – of scientists and technicians of university level, capable of selecting, adapting and repairing foreign technology. This focal point of highly trained scientists and engineers would combine know-how with what I call the all-important 'know who': up-to-date knowledge of those throughout the world who are advancing towards breakthroughs in solving problems that may confront a developing country: desertification, disease, and transport and energy problems.

Economic competition requires efficiency and quality. It is the universities that must develop these capacities, in cooperation with research and technology development centres and the productive sector, both nationally and, as in the industrialized countries, through international networks and twinning arrangements. The university is both the avant-garde institution which anticipates and the institution that provides critical, impartial analyses of society. If basic education is above all learning to learn, then higher education is 'learning to initiate'. All countries, whatever their level of development, need managers and initiators. When we speak of talent as the great device both nationally and internationally, we should speak less of the brain drain and more of wasted brains, encouraging, on the one hand, the training of national professionals and, on the other, reinsertion in each country of those that have benefited from foreign grants and aid.

In several instances there has been a considerable increase in the percentages of the gross domestic product destined for basic education. However, the percentages earmarked for research and development, around 0.3–0.5 per cent, are between five and six times less than the investments made by the industrialized countries and represent, without doubt, the great difference existing between the countries which generate technology and those that are still condemned passively to consume it.

When we speak of the free market, as when we speak of free expression, we should consider whether all countries and individuals have access to it. In fact, there is no doubt that protectionism should be modified at both national and sub-regional levels, preferably through economic alliances, communities or consortiums, broadening – as the Carlsson group recommended – the participation of the developing countries in world commerce. Equitable prices – or a reasonable range of price fluctuation – must be established for the raw materials of the developing countries. Otherwise they will never be able to plan any credible national development strategy.

If certain guarantees are not established for the purchasing of basic products from developing countries, it will be very difficult to help their economic development in real terms. This is especially so given the prevailing norms – already completely out of tune with today's reality – relative to the payment of the foreign debt entered into more than 15 years ago by the developing countries. Not only do we need new, more imaginative formulae, capable of stimulating development in the Third World, but also we must consider writing off the foreign debt, at least in part, as being part of the price that has to be paid for peace. We must promote investment and share knowledge so that Third-World countries can store and eventually partially transform their raw materials.

Considerable amounts must be invested in order to avoid the degeneration of the environment. In this, as in other matters, we must be able to have a global vision of what one unit of energy costs, doing a thorough analysis of the *real* cost. We waste time on emotional or anecdotal considerations, which sometimes carry with them economic interests of extraordinary proportions. It should be added here that, when the price of coal is calculated, for example, we should not just take into account its worth from the economic point of view: not only the resulting products (that depend on the quality of the coal), not only the preparatory treatment that needs to be applied to prevent the emission of toxic gases, besides the carbon dioxide, but also the cost in human lives through mining disasters, silicosis and so on. The price of peace must not omit the prime factor; that is, the protagonist and beneficiary: each person, each man and each woman. It is not only in short-term economic terms, but in long-term investments in ecological terms, that 'the cost of living' must be defined.

In 1990, the Organization for Economic Cooperation and Development (OECD) countries produced around 9 billion tons of waste; 330 million people living in the 24 OECD countries dump untreated residual waste. The progress achieved in some countries in controlling the emission of toxic gases has yet to be perfected and, above all, such progress should be shared with other countries in which comparable technological possibilities do not exist. But it must be stated that these substances know no frontiers, that the wind and the sea know no national borders. Japan, which has in 20 years increased its gross domestic product by 116 per cent, has, over this same period, reduced its sulphur emissions (sulphur dioxide) by 80 per cent. None the less, technological perfection in controlling the emission of gases is inadequate compensation for the doubling or quadrupling of the number of vehicles. The same reflection applies in the case of intensive agriculture, which now produces enormous contamination of underground water through excessive use of nitrogenous fertilizers, pesticides and so on. Technology and science are needed in order to know *the exact treatment* that should be given to the land according to the harvests required, as is the technology which should be applied to different industries to avoid toxic gas emission and so on. However, these measures often meet fierce resistance. Only awareness that changes of all types can come about, changes that can irreversibly compromise the future in a very humanly perceptible time frame – that of our grandchildren or great-grand-children – could ensure the adoption of adequate measures in sufficient time. We must also take into account the enormous quantity of new substances that are produced each year with effects on the biosphere which cannot be calculated for several years to come.

The environment will be a decisive factor in foreign policy. There is no common foreign policy without a common policy on security, which until now, has involved preventing military confrontation between nations. Today security includes, above all, the environment, whose degradation is a less visible enemy but a more pernicious one than the most sophisticated weapons systems. The UN Conference on

Environment and Development (UNCED) which took place in Rio de Janeiro in 1992 constitutes an extraordinary milestone, planning for the environment as well as for development. The UN system, on behalf of the most relevant non-governmental organizations representing the scientific and technological community, made considerable progress in providing world leaders with the basic scientific elements. In Geneva, in October 1990, the Second World Conference on Climate Change was held. A group of more than 800 eminent scientists studied the report which had been drafted by the International Panel on Climate Change (IPCC) and, in a second phase, the 'scientific' conclusions were conveyed to the ministerial representatives for their consideration. Although it is true that certain countries were very reluctant in accepting many of the scientists' recommendations, I had the opportunity, on behalf of all the heads of the organizing agencies (World Meteorological Organization, UN Environment Programme, Food & Agriculture Organization, Intergovernmental Oceanographic Commission, International Council of Scientific Unions) to say a few words at the closing session: 'The importance of the first step, even if it is timid, is that it should be in the right direction.' Indeed, the climate questions were discussed seriously and with the necessary rigour, thus enabling UNCED to start out from a solid and promising basis.

The UN must develop adequate mechanisms in order for the necessary steps to be taken internationally to prevent the environment's degradation. The most important aspects should be discussed by the Security Council, duly advised by the specialized agencies, and the practical application of the measures decided upon could be carried out under the supervision of technicians working on these matters in the service of the UN (the 'green helmets', together with the blue helmets, would be the keepers of ecological peace and peace among nations).

Only 100 years ago, 90 per cent of energy came from wood. Today 70 per cent comes from gas and oil combustion. We must be aware that oil represents – will represent – the main energy source for an extraordinarily short space of time: in 40, 50 or 100 years, at the most, it is reckoned that there will be no more reserves. Coal reserves are predicted to run out around the year 2300. None the less, we are surrounded by forms of energy which do not produce toxic waste: wind energy, tidal energy and photosynthetic energy. The great problem is storing energy produced from these sources and putting that energy to use. Thus it is difficult to imagine at the moment the replacement of combustibles for air transport, but for road transport, especially in the cities, electric energy from storage batteries can be supplied by photovoltaic mechanisms. Solar energy constitutes an alternative that we must continue to explore, through the necessary investments in R&D. After all, in the final analysis, wood, like coal and oil, is created by the effect of solar energy on water (photolysis of the water molecule) because of the action of the chlorophyll green pigment.

It is all a question of attitude. The possibility of a nuclear war was beyond the control of individual citizens. Such a catastrophe would have been the result of decisions taken by the two super powers. The environment, on the other hand, can be brought into equilibrium by the actions of each of us: citizens in each country have their part to play. We can all ensure that the environment will be preserved so that future generations can fully enjoy life on the planet. In fact, it is not a question of man and the biosphere, but rather of man *in* the biosphere, of how he can live in a specific physical context. These attitudes are generated through education. There should be instruction on the environment from the first years of schooling through to university level.

The population problem presents itself in all spheres: ecological, social, political, family life and so on. We often forget that the new Europe, unmutilated Europe, has in all around 600 million inhabitants. This is two-thirds of India's population and approximately half of China's. The indices of demographic growth and the ensuing migration flows should also be taken into account. At the moment the population increase is not due to greater fertility but greater survival rates. The mortality and disease rates have fallen, thanks to vaccinations, the use of antibiotics and so on. This shows us that *development is indivisible*: we cannot just help people to survive but we must also help them to be fed, clothed and housed – and to be educated. I believe the agreement reached at the 1990 World Summit for Children was an important turning-point in development thinking because it comprises three basic pillars: sanitation, nutrition and education. For similar reasons, I decided to propose three main focuses for all UNESCO's activities for the 1994–95 biennium: women, Africa and the least developed countries. In the Maghreb, the results of education for women have been spectacular: in ten years, not only basic education but also secondary and higher education have improved, and the birth rate has dropped by 50 per cent. Education is the solution!

In some countries the population has doubled in 14 or 15 years which means that half the citizens are children and adolescents. Many people live their lives without setting foot outside their immediate locality in many countries of the world! Young people in the developing countries have to face the immediate problems of survival, of finding a way to a better financial situation, of obtaining housing, food and clean water. In contrast, in the cities and in the more favoured social classes, there are so many young people who have almost everything and are unaware of the cost because they have not needed to exert the slightest effort in obtaining these 'consumer tools'.

Yet for all the young, rich and poor, another danger born of desperation, despair and even boredom, exists. It is another of the great threats to peace in the world and it should, therefore, be eradicated:

drugs. Instead of imposing rules and criteria on young people, we must set good examples. In 'The Prophet', Khalil Gibran writes with regard to our children:

Their souls dwell in the house of tomorrow
Which you cannot visit, not even in your dreams …
You may strive to be like them, but seek not to make them like you
For life goes not backward …

In Spain, in 1988, 249 young people died of an overdose; in 1989, statistics indicate 579 – the figure had more than doubled. In the first four months of 1990, 56 young people died in Madrid; again, the cause of death was an overdose. These are shattering figures. Today drugs are the great pandemic and drug-traffickers are our worst enemies.

An Inter-American Development Bank report, published recently in Chile, indicates that around 20 million children live in the streets of Latin America and the Caribbean. The majority take 'legal' or 'illegal' drugs. Many of these young children inhale solvents such as glue or petrol, which have an irreversible impact on brain function. The number of those smoking marijuana has increased enormously. They say they take drugs 'so as not to feel the cold'. The two extremes, extreme poverty and availability of too much, too soon, lead to drug-taking. The traffic of these substances has increased, the Secretary General of the United Nations informed us at the Ministerial Summit on Drugs (London, 9–11 April 1990), reaching a market value of 500 000 million dollars a year. This bonanza is only exceeded by international arms sales. It is reckoned that there are 41 million illicit drug-takers, but obviously, it is not a question of economic magnitude but rather of human lives, especially of young lives. With drugs, as with armaments, demand should be considered simultaneously with supply.

The least developed countries, being the weakest, are those that pay the most for the armed conflicts or economic crises of other, more affluent parts of the world. The Conference on the Least Developed Countries (organized by the United Nations) which took place at UNESCO in September 1990 concluded that urgent measures of external aid – both economic and in human resources – were needed, including the rapid promotion of education and other services. The poorest countries have suffered enormously from the effects of structural re-adjustments made by international financial institutions during the last decade, including severe cutbacks in educational, health and other investments in future well-being. The price of peace surely includes measures to promote basic development, including human resource development. For their own safety, to avoid problems rooted in poverty, such as fanaticism and mass immigration, the rich countries should increase aid for national development of the least developed countries, to reach 3–3.5 per cent of GDP. We cannot apply to the less developed countries the political, economic and financial conditions that are applied to highly industrialized countries. Thus, in many cases, privatization is equivalent to placing domestic industry in foreign hands; outside investors will take what the weak domestic private sector cannot absorb: 'You can't privatize when there is nothing to privatize', a brilliant African told me recently. 'Europe cannot pretend that its procedures and models are applicable without any adaptation to different cultural and economic contexts.' Therefore we should consider the social consequences of structural adjustment.

Paying the price of peace! It costs far less than war, but we are not ready for peace: we do not invest in rapid and efficient ways of protecting ourselves from fire, flood or natural disasters; we do not invest in development aid for neighbouring countries who would then become our allies and our markets. Instead, we feel threatened by violence; violence brought about by their living conditions. We do not invest in teaching all people of all ages, 'reaching the unreachable' through the communication means at our disposal. We just keep going, without wanting to see the 250 000 people who arrive on our planet each day, most of them in the poorest countries. We do not want to see beyond our immediate locality, or any further than the borders of our country. We do not take the drastic steps needed to be rid of the unbearable shame of the 'street children'; instead, we celebrate with great pomp the 'International Year of the Family'.

In order to pay the price of peace we do not have to look outside. The solution does not lie elsewhere, in another country, but in every single country. Foreign aid can unlock and help to release existing funds and be a guide in the development process. The price of peace is not paid solely by national administrations or international institutions. It is paid with the everyday behaviour of each one of us. And that behaviour – as I have already said – is the ultimate expression of culture.

Note

1   The Carlsson group referred to here was a study group chaired by former Swedish Prime Minister Carlsson. The group published a report: "Common Responsibility in the 1990s. The Stockholm Initiative on Global Security and Governance". (Published in Stockholm in 1991.

7 Changing Perspectives

Life is a constant series of transitions. As the proverb says, time and tide wait for no man. We are neither the masters of history nor its slaves. Nor are we the masters of nature, as science once taught us. We are part of systems in which we can play a very important role but in which the conditions of action are not set entirely by us. Past generations, past decisions, present patterns have all essentially rigged the game in one direction or another, limiting and partially influencing the kinds of action which we must take. We do not begin, therefore, from a *tabula rasa*. Our action must be goal-oriented but at the same time clearly rooted in the realities and possibilities of the present.

As a scientist, a scholar, a teacher and a politician, I have found that transitions in my own life are best mastered by taking each experience as an opportunity to grow and grapple with new demands on my training and qualities. As anyone who has taught or administered a large university with thousands of students watching your every move, or as anyone who has been in public life knows, one will always face the risk of making mistakes and one will always have the opportunity for rather comic or tragic trips, stumbles or falls.

Life has become increasingly complex in the present century, and the decisions we make are in greater need of a corrective, 'feedback' procedure. But the passion for life when we are dedicated to scientific research, or to developing democracy where it has not existed for a long time, or to reforming an international organization, is fundamentally a passion for persistence. It is a stubbornness based on anger or annoyance with the way things are. It requires an intellectual curiosity for finding ways of creating change where others feel that change is impossible. Uncertainty does not necessarily disappear with the input of more knowledge, since uncertainty is an essential component of the behaviour of complex systems. And man is the most complex of all.

This is the continual dialectic of the reformer, the impatient, the passionate with the faint-hearted. Indeed, the dialectic of modern life revolves to a great degree around this dyad of the seemingly romantic belief that things can be done and the cynical pose that not much is really possible and we should simply let things go on the way they always have. I detest and abhor indifference and fatalism. I believe the value systems for which science, education, culture and the freedom of information have been developed are real values with concrete meaning in our everyday lives. They are not posters or advertising slogans for outwardly acceptable but inwardly corrupt or ineffective people and institutions. We are ultimately responsible for the lives we build around us and if we are placed in positions of responsibility we remain historically the people who ought to be judged as to whether we have succeeded or failed in advancing the human project.

In Spanish civilization *Don Quixote* is often viewed from a cynical or off-putting perspective as a parable on man's ability to fool himself. Yet well-grounded and acute historical–literary criticism of Cervantes shows very clearly that he is describing to us the collapse of a social system based on the outworn values of chivalry, so dramatically and comically described in this, one of the first novels ever written. In fact, the first novels, of Cervantes or Richardson or any of the early pioneers of the prose form, are contemporary with the beginnings of science. The novel seeks to describe things as they are in ways which lead us to think about why they are the way they are and to try to come to grips with the way we as individuals reading the novel relate to that reality – just as the scientist is from the very beginning, from the time of Newton, trying to measure and understand nature and natural phenomena which have been looked at and experienced throughout human history. These early scientists tried for the first time to make predictive and quantified models showing what makes nature work. It is this modernist sense of finding the truth, unvarnished, unalloyed, unencrusted with baroque or rococo decoration that makes our era so fascinating. 20th-century modernism has pushed that even further because our science has moved beyond the mechanical to the beginnings of an understanding of the instabilities inherent in natural systems. Life is not linear. Life is uncertain and we are constantly dealing with probabilities based on not quite certain knowledge of what makes a phenomenon function. That of course includes ourselves, society around us and the world at large. Heraclitus was right: 'Everything flows and nothing stays.' And, therefore, freedom has bounds. Human life acquires meaning.

This does not mean that the scientist teaching in a medical faculty or the public affairs analyst teaching in a political science department should turn to his or her students and instantly proclaim that we do not know anything very well and therefore we should sit silently in our corner and let everything work out until we have a fuller understanding of things. That is not the nature of either the scientific or the humanitarian enterprise. From the time certainly of James Joyce,

Federico Garcia Llorca, Salvador Dali or Isadora Duncan, the 20th-century modernist impulse has been – long before Wittgenstein put it forward as a philosophical theory – that we use words and gestures and artistic representations of things which neither language nor shape can ever fully express. We are, nonetheless, still trying, within the necessarily limited means of communication that we have inherited from past generations, to say things that were perhaps taboo or to learn things that were considered not worth knowing or too dangerous to know. More important, we are attempting to transcend the loneliness of individual feelings and thoughts in highly individuated urban societies in ways which may be a mere shadow-play of the full texture of everything that we experience. It is, however, certainly better than silence.

This is why the younger generations, those of the 1920s scarred by the First World War, those of the 1940s and 1950s who survived the Second World War, and particularly those of the 1960s and thereafter, have placed such an importance on saying the complete, unvarnished truth. This passion for self-expression, which sometimes may be a way of expressing feelings so overwhelming that it does not really matter whether people listen or not, is also at its root a passion to be understood. And what has been lacking in modern societies, both in the wealthy and the poor countries, between generations and between all kinds of different groups has been perhaps the loss of patience and solace that can be afforded by simply listening and looking and experiencing the realities of others.

That is why my present role as Director-General of UNESCO has so far been one of the most exhilarating and challenging tests of my life. It is a truism that the world has been based on local, regional and national traditions of government and that things are organized historically around localities or national units. No-one at present is prepared for global responsibility where basically the entire world is one's constituency. The sheer scope of the communities one is addressing and the interrelatedness of the natural, social and educational problems they face is daunting enough. The strains of a world divided between a minority with a great deal of wealth and a majority very close to absolute poverty are dramatic.

The first part of learning the job of dealing at a global level with a range of questions is simply to see how other people live and think and express themselves in many places one has never been and in many situations one has never experienced. It is said by some who criticize my travelling that I am out of my office in Paris too much. Perhaps. I personally feel that the director-general of a world institution operating at educational levels that run from pre-school to university, at communication levels that run from the smallest rural mimeographed newspaper to great national colour television networks, with scientific establishments ranging from those that sometimes lack the most basic equipment to those that are pushing against the barriers of what can be done in big science, needs to see, feel and touch the concrete specificities of many local situations. No-one on taking up such duties could ever say with any credibility that he or she was stepping into global functions which could be carried out on the basis of a theoretical knowledge of education, science, culture or communication among all the 182 member states of a world organization. No human being has lived long enough or seen enough or been in a position to confront these issues at all their levels to the extent of being an expert from a global perspective. One can be as expert as can be nationally or regionally or in terms of mastering one's discipline in the sciences, the social sciences or humanities, but one can never argue that one arrives at such functions on the basis of a full and effective knowledge of what happens throughout the world. Our biographies and our educational backgrounds are simply not global in scope, although we live in a world in which the global has more and more of an impact on what happens to us in our local lives.

My job is not an administrative one. I depend on trained administrators to carry out the policy decisions that I must make as director-general. My job is to lead UNESCO with its member states towards being a more effective contributor in solving global problems in its areas of expertise. I travel to villages in the jungle or the desert or to national capitals in both the poorest and the richest countries in order to develop a perspective on what my organization could best be doing. This cannot be done in the abstract environment of headquarters. Indeed, my entire policy at UNESCO has been to put the organization more and more in contact with the realities of everyday life in the multivarious settings of the world as it is. That is especially the task of an international organization that has a responsibility to help countries of all kinds to work better in millions of classrooms, to work better in thousands of laboratories, to work better in hundreds of artists', cinema and television studios. Each of these are part of a set of global realities which cannot be grasped by homogenization or by abstraction.

As a young biochemist I had the privilege of working in the Metabolic Research Laboratories of Professor Krebs, at Oxford. His workstyle was never to ask the very specific speciality out of which one had come to his laboratory. He knew what kind of work you were interested in doing as part of the general, biological research that took place on the projects he was engaged in. He used to say that the job of a scientist was to see things that lots of people had already seen and to understand them in ways no-one had before. Indeed, when he retired, this great Nobel laureate left his laboratory to continue under the guidance of his chief laboratory technician who, an extraordinarily skilled scientist, had never had the time or the opportunity to amass a series of higher degrees. What concerned Krebs was whether one could do the work and whether one had the liveliness of mind and the practical ability to find things in the biological world that others may have only learned of or kept in touch with through books. Degrees and specialities were less important to him, and to me, than the ability to think and pose problems and find solutions. There is no theoretical or book-learning way that can constitute that kind of direct practical knowledge. Observation is the basis of all science and, I would argue, of all knowledge.

That is why from the very outset I have conceived of UNESCO, even in the crisis of the withdrawal, prior to my election, of the United States, the United Kingdom and Singapore, as an organization with the responsibility of moving forward and of making itself a better and better watchtower for the world of learning and for the professions engaged in research, teaching, culture and communications. UNESCO exists to help all these intellectual and cultural professionals to understand better the trends in the world around them. As such, it is also of course a watchtower for decision makers, enabling them to get the best available advice, the most up-to-date information and analyses on which they can base their policy judgements.

In the secretariat of UNESCO itself I am doing all that I can to take down the bureaucratic barriers between different specialities that are all working on related problems. I hope that UNESCO's training programmes help others experience the passion of applying intellectual rigour to problem solving. I believe that the solutions to many of the problems of the present, however difficult, are within our grasp. For those which still elude us, we can at least begin to pose the problems in such a way as to focus research and resources on finding solutions.

I will not be content with a UNESCO which remains purely a governmental ministry of education, science, culture and communication on a global scale because, as much as I recognize the importance and difficult work of such government bureaucracies, I also recognize that the founders of UNESCO wanted the organization to go beyond the questions of political decision making to open itself up to the very newest and the most challenging work being carried out in all its fields of competence. Advances in our knowledge are being made by scholars and specialists every day. Some are old and distinguished, others are young and iconoclastic. Rarely are they found in government offices. Therefore, I believe, by becoming a kind of agora of the most interesting, difficult, far-reaching work in its fields, UNESCO, like the great universities, could automatically be of increased value to the global society in which it works. As an international intellectual and teaching organization, it must be open to all who have new or good solutions to propose to the problems facing decision makers and public alike.

For this, UNESCO must take on the functions of being a direct and responsive resource for men and women everywhere who are involved in research, creativity, teaching and communicating. And, with modern telecommunications and the development of rapid and inexpensive ways of transmitting information back and forth, UNESCO could certainly develop into a kind of global university and institute of advanced study without walls which is at the same time accessible to the most advanced thinkers in certain subjects and to those who teach these subjects at all levels.

Science, the humanities, philosophy, poetry and access to information cannot remain affairs of governments. Governments have much that they can do in legislation and in investment to support those kinds of activities, but it is the practitioners in the freedom of their laboratories, in the pressures and challenges of their classrooms and studios and editorial offices who together carry out the work of teaching, learning, research and reporting that exemplifies the intellectual cooperation and progress that is possible on a world scale.

Let us begin at a very micro level and then deal with a much more global phenomenon. Tens of millions of children in the developing countries will never have the opportunity to go to school if the present level of investment is maintained. Some of them cannot attend school simply because their parents cannot afford a simple ballpoint pen or an exercise book. One of my best memories as Director-General of UNESCO – a memory coloured by both humility and disbelief – is of hearing education ministers present me with an urgent request for blackboards, chalk, pens and paper. Had I heard them correctly? They were not asking for schools, or professional training teams, or textbooks – no, just pencils and paper! It reminded me of a poem I had written one day, somewhere:

> How many desks, classrooms,
> books, openings,
> could those guns be worth!
> thousands of soldiers file by
> and burnished armoured cars
> while millions
> live bowed down, on bended knee
> they keep imploring us to have
> the courage to end the farce
> and, finally, let them stand.

And so I thought that the best way for children from wealthy countries to be made aware of the difference between themselves and those of the poorer countries was for they themselves to supply those basic materials. In a small experiment at UNESCO, and in France, because that is where we are located and where we can try out such an approach most easily, we have arranged with pen manufacturers, the Reynolds company, and with various suppliers of exercise books to provide, at cost, a pen and an exercise book for a child in a developing country for ten francs, which is about one pound sterling or two dollars. This kind of direct help, so practical and so needed, has two purposes. First it meets an obvious and crying need that enables a young person in a very poor country and from a very poor background to go to school. But it also teaches the children here, in the industrialized world, that they can help, with a little of their pocket money, a brother or sister in some far-off place to have some of the chances and some of the opportunities that they may take for granted. It is a way of bringing the reality of the poverty and sometimes the hopelessness of the developing countries home to a new generation of schoolchildren in the world's north. I hope that there are others, including readers of this book, who will help me in this very basic kind of campaign. Each of us, at our local levels, could see to it that other schoolchildren in other parts of the world – rich and poor – can also participate in some direct fashion in what is a basic factor in global development, the education of all the children.

From a larger, but no more abstract perspective, it should be understood that in some countries of the developing world the population is literally doubling every seven years. That means that more than half the population in these countries is under the age of 25 and a significant number of these have never been to school. Their chances of employment, of self-expression and of being real contributors to their societies have perhaps been handicapped for ever. What are we to expect of them when the despair and the suffering, and perhaps the hunger, lead to explosions of fundamentalist or terrorist rage against the 'happy few'? So UNESCO is working to provide, not only basic education for the children, but also vocational, technical and continuing education to adolescent and adult school-leavers. So that nobody feels they have missed the boat with regard to education, and that everyone at any age can have access to all levels of education, there are two basic conditions to be met: continuous, intensive courses and 'deformalization' of the education process – doing away with equivalence tests, so that everyone may have the possibility of taking up any type of study without first of all having to present earlier study diplomas and so on. With the modern means of communication at our disposal, distance learning will be able to reach out to those who live in isolated settlements. And, as I have written above, education of women is the most effective way to reduce population growth and ensure that children are educated.

The privileged in the wealthier countries, or for that matter the privileged in many of the world's poorer countries, where there are enclaves of wealth equivalent to that experienced in the north, may not fully understand what it means to have literally no options for self-improvement because one has been born poor. This is a question which in many societies has led to major social changes involving access to education and especially to higher education in the period after the Second World War. If we cannot extend the same set of concerns to children outside our own personal experiences or even outside our own national setting, the world itself stands to lose. We are part of that world and we will also be the losers. The problem here is empathy, love, the ability to put oneself, with some difficulty and certainly with some pain, in the situation experienced day by day by others far away either perceptually or geographically.

I have had the privilege and the pain of seeing the street children of many cities, in countries rich and poor. Deprived of the nurture and support of a father and mother, let loose to be the prey of the most decadent forces one can imagine in any society, they are the reserve army of crime, 'targets of opportunity' for those who recruit new generations for drugs, prostitution and violence. They are the victims of neglect and degradation of societies which have turned their back on those who are most vulnerable. Only a culture of war can accept this as 'the nature of things'. I hope that the communications media of the world, the child development specialists and those who can describe with feeling and authority what this level of suffering and despair means to a seven- or eight-year-old child can somehow bring that image home to the public and the decision makers. Only then will the necessary resources be focused on helping families, communities and educational systems to stem the tide of lost children who, preyed upon by others at an early age, will become feral adults. Street children, children forced to work, exploited, inhaling glue and solvents – how can we reconcile all this with the dream? The situation is in our hands, in those of each citizen, in those of each municipality, to find a way to rid ourselves of this collective shame within a matter of months. Yes, months. We must not acquire one more plane, or construct another stretch of motorway; we must not simply let everything go on as usual and only half-heartedly help those children excluded from our society. We must invest in the enterprise of justice and love *instead of* investing in other aspects of routine life that occasionally make us think, with cowardice and apathy, that for some things there is no remedy. Street children must be able to find a hand stretched out to them in the coming months. Otherwise, it is clear that, once again, empty words and well-meant yet irrelevant action will be wasting ethical space where all that is wanted is justice.

Science is another area which seems quite abstract but is one where we can begin from the simplest and most practical of problem-solving approaches. The scientific faculties of the poorest countries have little access to the literature and research opportunities available in the great research institutions of the wealthier countries. That often means that a high school student in these countries will feel discouraged from pursuing a scientific or technological career. Talent in these fields offers so many possible benefits to a country seeking to improve its agricultural and industrial productivity. This is, after all, one of the most basic inputs and investments in the development process. Vast telecommunication networks now allow for academic research and interaction to take place on a scale unthinkable only a few years ago. UNESCO will continue this kind of simple, practical twinning, sharing the inspired teaching and guidance of great scientists with places where they are only names or signatures in textbooks.

These are seemingly small and certainly not very expensive measures. They require an ability to innovate, a willingness to seek funding sources, or sources of talent and energy in many different kinds of institutions and settings. That is the commitment of UNESCO and of all members of the scientific and educational community, to permit the sharing of talent and the encouragement of talent wherever it may be found. Today's world, more than ever, needs talent and tenacity to solve unforeseen problems in often unexpected places. We are ready for any threats to national sovereignty, but we are not ready to face dangers hovering over us. We must radically change our ways to obtain the best from our richest resource – the abilities of everyone on the planet.

In cultures of democracy – because there are many – in societies willing to pay the price of peace, these are the kinds of practical measures that citizens can take at very local levels. Central to such an enterprise are schoolteachers, librarians, scientists, technicians, administrators, bankers, philanthropists and foundations. All can participate in such a series of practical activities to spread knowledge and the passion for learning where it has not been able to go before. This is a way of building a democratic spirit of enquiry and of constructing the defences of freedom which are also the defences of peace in the minds of people everywhere.

It has very often been said, and perhaps must be said again and again, that we who live together on the Earth at the present time must learn to share it better. Much of that means not so much sharing our wealth as sharing our knowledge and experience, expertise and energy with others. These are not major changes in our lifestyle but the beginnings of ways to a perhaps more austere, more conscious, more globally connected way of seeing and doing things that have an impact on today's world for tomorrow's generations.

When in the early 1960s I was involved in post-doctoral studies on the west coast of the United States, I remember that a number of political movements, including students and faculty members, and racial minorities living in the slums of the great cities, proposed a slogan that said: 'If you are not part of the solution, you are part of the problem.'

UNESCO was founded by an even older generation which believed in much the same idea, that working together to find solutions to educational, cultural and scientific problems was the way to progress with the most humanistic of enterprises: working to help the whole species evolve towards freedom, democracy and peace.

Julian Huxley proposed his philosophy of evolutionary humanism as UNESCO's unique outlook on the world before he was elected the organization's first director-general. And this courageous, even controversial 'profession de foi' probably cost Huxley a reduction in his term of office, from the statutory six years to two. He accepted this as the price for doing what must be done if an international intellectual organization is to live up to its promise: its leadership must be free to speak out on the issues of the day and link them with UNESCO's missions in education, science, culture and communications. It is the very essence of the culture of democracy that the world of ideas and research and the world of politics and problem solving must never be permitted to drift apart. They must exist in a co-equal, uncomfortable tension if the future is to be seen in all its promise and dangers and if the human species is to move towards realizing its deepest ethical and aesthetic values.

Brought up in the heat of theological and ideological controversy about Darwin's *Evolution of the Species*, Julian Huxley was a biologist with deep roots in the democratic tradition of Utilitarianism. His forebear, T.H. Huxley, was a fierce debater for Darwinian principles and a scientific wit. He once retorted to Bishop Samuel Wilberforce:

> I asserted – and I repeat – that a man has no reason to be ashamed of having an ape for his grandfather. If there were an ancestor whom I should feel shame in recalling it would rather be a man ... who, not content with an equivocal success in his own sphere of activity, plunges into scientific questions with which he has no real acquaintance.

He also wrote, 'The great tragedy of Science – the slaying of a beautiful hypothesis by an ugly fact.'

Julian Huxley saw UNESCO as a new movement in the upward spiral of human evolution: to greater complexity, global thinking and personal growth for all. Allowing for the fact that he wrote *UNESCO: Its Purpose and Its Philosophy* more than a generation ago, Huxley's general approach remains a reasoned and passionate call to action for UNESCO as a builder of peace and a culture of democracy. He wrote:

> Of special importance in man's evaluation of his own position in the cosmic scheme and of his further destiny is the fact that he is the heir, and indeed the sole heir, of evolutionary progress to date ... Furthermore, he is not merely the sole heir of past evolutionary progress, but the sole trustee for any that may be achieved in the future. From the evolutionary point of view, the

destiny of man may be summed up very simply: it is to realize the maximum progress in the minimum of time. That is why the philosophy of UNESCO must have an evolutionary background and why the concept of progress cannot but occupy a central position in that philosophy. (p.12)

In arguing that democratic values must guide the new organization, Huxley added:

UNESCO cannot be neutral in the face of competing values. Even if it were to refuse to make a conscious choice among them, it would find that the necessity for action involved such a choice, so that it would be driven eventually to the unconscious assumption of a system of values. And any such system which is unconsciously assumed is less likely to be true than one which is consciously sought after and studied ... There are still ethical values which are general and lasting – namely those which promote a social organization which will allow individuals the fullest opportunity for development and self-expression consonant with the persistence and progress of society.

These values necessitated hard work and deep feelings for UNESCO's first director-general: 'Our ethical systems to-day are still largely predicated on a pre-scientific and nationally fragmented world. We have to relate them to our new knowledge and our new closeness to each other.'

With remarkable prescience, Huxley concluded by wondering if UNESCO could truly serve the world community in an atmosphere of impending cold war, but – in 1946! – he wrote:

Two opposing philosophies of life confront each other from the West and from the East, and not only impede the achievement of unity but threaten to become the foci of actual conflict ... Can this conflict be avoided, these opposites be reconciled, this antithesis be resolved in a higher synthesis? I believe not only that this can happen, but that through the inexorable dialectic of evolution, it must happen – only I do not know whether it will happen before or after another war.

If I ever get the chance to brief my predecessor in the hereafter, I will have to admit that, more than a generation later, the cold war and other related events certainly did prevent UNESCO from achieving many of the hopes that Huxley and other founders shared. But I could also confirm that evolution has indeed largely ended the division of the world into hostile camps and that, at the end of this century, UNESCO is moving towards its 'rendezvous with destiny'. And that destiny is democracy, active, direct participation of citizens exercising their individual freedoms and unique talents in solving global problems. As the problems that we face force us to think globally merely to understand what we experience locally, and as the barriers of our cultures of war open up to reveal new perspectives on our common stake in the global common, each of us can contribute to turning a new page in Earth' s history.

The transformation begins, as always, within. As each of us can begin to realize that the war culture celebrates violence as strength and views poetry as weakness, and as we can see within us the terrible wounds we carry from the 'mobilization mentality', each of us can be an agent of change. Power will always need thought, 'mind supplements', because it is all too often overloaded and bogged down in the immediate. Democracy' s critics, those who prefer a military and dogmatic discipline to freedom, have always derided its defenders as weaklings in their tolerance of debate and dissent, as effeminate in their concern for the welfare of the poor, the sick and the disabled, and as pettifogging in their scrupulous respect for the rule of law. The reverse has always been true: the men and women who built and continue to build democratic cultures are strong in their individuality, confident in their male or female gender, sensitive to their responsibilities towards new generations and courageous in their quest for laws that promote 'liberty and justice for all'.

Because democratic leadership is a form of teaching ethical values and their role in public policy, it must rigorously seek the truth and sometimes harshly debunk cynical and ignorant myths. UNESCO, therefore, like a university, or an institute for advanced studies, will always say or do things that trouble those wedded to dogma, to ignorance or to prejudice. If it is to be of value to the member states and the communities it exists to serve, it must 'speak the truth to Power' when the best minds and the current 'state of the art' clearly indicate where the truth may lead. To revitalize UNESCO and make it more relevant and more accessible to those working in its fields, its director-general and its staff must constantly keep in mind that, to be an effective leader, one must be prepared to serve.

If any international organization needs to be in a permanent state of rethinking and relearning, it is UNESCO. It cannot be a faceless, thoughtless, insensitive and routinized bureaucracy. Each unit of the secretariat must be alert and curious about new developments in its field: new insights, new approaches and new generations of scholars, scientists, artists and professionals must always bring our programmes and our staff up to date. The world of ideas, of teaching and learning, can advance education, science, culture and communication into what Huxley called the 'dark spaces' of poverty and ignorance only by the power of knowledge and the force of persuasion.

UNESCO itself must become a community of thinkers and doers who transcend their specialities and the habits of the past to gain a global perspective on problems and the opportunity to work with and for those who suffer from lack of access to education, to the benefits of science and the solace of culture. Not all will be poets, but poetry must move them all. Not all will be scientists, but all will be precise. Not all will be teachers, but all will share an enthusiasm to express the excitement of learning.

We are indeed complex creatures, with a brain and a consciousness perched on top of a set of organs and functions we share with the rest of the animal kingdom. Only we can know that we are also perched on a tiny speck of dust on an outer branch of the Milky Way and that our species has existed for a relatively brief moment in the physical history of the universe. Only we add love to lust in the biological world and it is love that permits us to reach out to others, banish time and transcend death. Throughout the world, the best of us can feel the pain of starvation and suffering of others and translate the agony of feeling into the pleasure of finding ways and means to improve the quality of human life. Often the first step to a solution is in words, ways of trying to express and describe and communicate to others the suffering of strangers, or the beauty of a ruin or the danger of impending drought. Such words are actions and UNESCO's future is intimately related to the power of words to vector our thoughts and our feelings from the local to the global and from the past to the future.

As I write, I realize that Christmas will soon be here, and I think of all the religions of the world that posit rebirth as the dawning of a state of grace. Grace is always wisdom and always love, because it is visible in the justice of our acts and the meaning of our lives. I think of the street children and other youngsters who will sleep 'hard', unloved and unfed tonight, and I realize that, if I can attain a state of grace, it will not be a passive peacefulness, but a sense of terrible, clear knowledge of what must be done and how quickly. To cross the great divide from a war culture that accepts chronic injustice as the price of war and move toward a culture of peace based on the dignity of each man, woman and child will require immense efforts. But words count, and I have written these words in the belief that words are beginnings of actions and that 'In the beginning was the Word.'

8 No Business as Usual!

When I first began working on the concept of the *The New Page* the Soviet Union still existed, the Berlin wall still stood, Europe remained divided and only the first steps backward from nuclear confrontation had been taken. The bipolar, cold war shape of the world has changed from the confrontation of superpowers to many points of violent, ethnic or religious conflict in the former Soviet Union, in the successor states of Yugoslavia and in Africa and the Middle East. At the same time, chronic problems, often masked by the cold war, have come into sharper relief: poverty, ignorance, threats to human rights and democracy, mass migrations within and between countries, and the environment. Certainly the root of many of them is unbridled population growth in the poorest countries.

Today the United Nations system is trying to come to the fore as a forum for new, more decisive approaches to human resource development (the Thailand Conference on Education for All, in Jomtien in 1990 and the continuing follow-up), to questions of environment and development (the UNCED Conference in Rio de Janeiro in 1992), human rights (the 1993 Human Rights Conference in Vienna) and the crucial linkage between education (particularly of women and girls) and population (the 1993 New Delhi meeting of the leaders of the nine most populous countries). Moreover, United Nations peace-keeping has shifted dramatically from acting as a buffer on 'green' or 'blue' lines in places as disparate as Cyprus, Gaza and Lebanon to significant interventions in the Gulf, El Salvador, Cambodia, Bosnia and Somalia.

These fundamental changes in the role of international organizations could not have come about without an end to the divisions and tensions that marked the post-Second World War era: the geopolitical division of Europe and much of the world, the balance of nuclear terror which most of the world could only watch as helpless spectators, the need for most of the newly independent countries of the Third World to try to assert their sovereignty and development needs in an ideologically divided world, and the 'totalitarian temptation' held out by the propaganda of the communist world as an alternative to democratic and economic pluralism.

Yet, if the world we knew so well in the years after 1945 has changed radically and rapidly, we remain uncertain and unclear on the outline of things to come. Certainly, the shaping of a New World Order or, as I prefer to put it, diverse and plural 'new world orders' has hardly begun. The points of political hope are impressive: the liberation of Kuwait by forces acting under UN authority, the fragile peace in Central America, the rise of multi-party democracy throughout Latin America and the former communist bloc in Central and Eastern Europe, the successful UN efforts to end the Cambodian civil war, progress in the negotiations in South Africa which have paved the way for a non-racialist, democratic system, and the mutual recognition of Israel and the PLO. Yet the points of political concern, even alarm, are also dramatic: continuing ethnic violence in Bosnia and Somalia, civil war and starvation in Sudan, attacks on immigrants by neo-Nazi youths in Germany and the rise of fundamentalist intolerance within and between religious communities in many regions.

Change is essential. We can be its victims, its passive recipients, its 'dependent variables', or we can, with effort, become agents of change and writers of our own 'history of the future'. The rapid, often unexpected political developments of the past few years show clearly that political change can make it appear as if history were accelerating, yet underlying, unchanging factors remain obstacles to more deep-rooted change. The transformation of economic systems, even undertaken with great skill and perseverance, is much slower indeed. Witness the slow pace of economic change in the former communist countries, with its attendant threats to nascent democracy. We must beware of asking people who have lived under a tyranny that provided a margin, however meagre, of economic and social security to identify freedom with insecurity and misery. The chronic impoverishment of the least developed countries and of many communities in both the 'developed' and developing world is a continuing obstacle to democracy and to peace.

Cultural change, the transformation of our own values and attitudes, has been even slower than economic processes, lagging far behind political events: 'ethnic cleansing' in Bosnia, tribal warfare in Somalia and elsewhere, clashes between communities in the former Soviet Union and, perhaps worst of all, the curious passivity of those in the affluent societies of Western Europe and North America who could have acted sooner and more effectively to prevent the carnage. Those of us privileged to live in democratic, industrialized societies can hardly preach democracy and peaceful coexistence to warring ethnic factions, even in Europe itself, if we cannot mobilize our own conscience and our own considerable means to prevent violence and foster peaceful solutions to these conflicts. With all the immense respect we owe to those working for peace on the spot in Bosnia and Somalia, we can only note that, through no fault of their own, their arrival was unjustifiably delayed, especially in Somalia, where the grievous situation turned in favour of the warlords.

In his *Agenda for Peace*, Secretary-General Boutros Boutros-Ghali calls for a preventive approach (diplomatic and other efforts that can be deployed prior to the outbreak of conflict) which could help avoid the enormous costs of peace-keeping activities. This is what I have described as 'peace-building': efforts through education, culture and communication to promote a civic culture of civility that resolves conflicts through tolerance and persuasion. Yet, though we spend billions on peace-keeping forces, we provide 1 per cent or less for building schools, publishing books and promoting independent news media and other fundamental props to building peace in zones of actual or potential conflict.

The *Agenda for Peace* and the notion of peace building reflect the aspirations of those who founded the United Nations and UNESCO almost 50 years ago. They emerged from the horrors of the Second World War and the celebration of intolerance, irrationality and violence as 'pragmatic dreamers', determined to mobilize humanism and reason as forces for peace and security. As Dag Hammarskjöld put it in 1960, on the fifteenth anniversary of the foundation of the United Nations:

> On his road from conflict and emotion to reconciliation in this final hymn of praise, Beethoven [in the Ninth Symphony] has given us a confession and a credo which we, who work within and for this Organization, may well make our own. We take part in the continuous fight between different interests and ideologies, which so far has marked the history of humanity, but we may never lose our faith that the first movements one day will be followed by the fourth movement ... Inspired by that faith we try to impose the laws of the human mind and the integrity of the human will on the dramatic evolution in which we are all engaged.

For that faith and that dream, he gave his life.

But those world leaders who came together to found the United Nations and UNESCO, those 'pragmatic dreamers' who glimpsed a future outside the paradigm of the Second World War and the cold war are gone. We, who are actually living the post-cold war experience, seem to lack the vision, courage and impatience of that generation to strive for the harmony and hope of the 'Ode to Joy'. Instead of leaders, we all too often have 'managers', more concerned with the 'how' than the 'why' of things. Perhaps the vast enterprises required by the culture of war have led us to narrow our focus from the aims of what we do, or should be doing, to the machinery by which any number of goals, good or bad, can most efficiently be attained. Of course management, cost effectiveness and efficiency are important in all enterprises, private and public. But they are means to ends, not ends in themselves. As the Chinese proverb puts it, 'When a finger points to the moon, only the near-sighted look at the finger!'

In *Leadership*, James MacGregor Burns describes 'political management' as a loss of the ethical compass of government. If political leadership – and its 'managers' – base their actions only on winning elections, they will offer no new vision and challenge to the voters. By 'going with the flow' of the polling data, candidates and office holders trade courage and leadership for short-term gain. The community, the nation and the international system are the losers if 'leaders' cater to the prejudices of the electorate and flinch from sharing disturbing truths with their fellow citizens. Indeed, as Burns points out, the political candidate and the successful office holder are, at their best, teachers who can summon a community to recognize and confront problems. Confronting myth and prejudice, and changing people's attitudes are hardly prescriptions for easy popularity, but passivity and soothsaying in the midst of dangers is a formula for disaster.

Inaction, delay and silence have, however, characterized too many of our responses to the opportunities and dangers of our times. How many mayors of cities and towns have summoned their citizens to care for the homeless, reach out to the immigrant, or give a chance to the young seeking their first job? How many leaders at local levels have sought 'environment-friendly' solutions to problems of transport, waste and energy? Much of the distrust now expressed in the polls towards traditional parties in democratic systems reflects a rejection of 'politically managed' passivity and 'business as usual' at the local level, which is the only political arena for the great majority of people.

In the new democracies especially, but also in well-established democratic systems, pluralism and tolerance will survive or fail according to the success or otherwise of local government in solving community problems. This is so for two important reasons: the habits and attitudes of local political leadership are the school for future national leaders, as well as the 'vote-getting' machine for current national party or government leaders. Moreover, we live our lives, form, express and change out attitudes – our culture – in the concrete reality of our localities. It is in our neighbourhoods, villages and towns that our children receive their formal education as well as their first expe-riences of culture in the broadest sense. Will that local community teach tolerance, pluralism and democracy by example? Will it promote a sense of personal security and responsibility in dealing with its own problems of poverty, exclusion, drug abuse and other issues through effective community programmes in education, housing, town planning, culture and leisure? Will it provide a sound local base for experiencing and influencing national and international events?

If the political culture at the level of everyday life teaches the opposite of the high ideals embodied in democratic constitutions and political programmes, then democracy itself is at risk. The culture of democracy means citizen involvement and participation in taking decisions which affect community life. This requires leaders, local and national, who are willing to put their ethics and concerns to an electoral test and risk losing on the basis of the ideas and aims they put forward, rather than winning through 'campaign management'. Describing this latter form of contentless campaigning, the Reverend Martin Luther King spoke of politicians in these terms: 'The tendency of most is to adopt a view that is so ambiguous that it will include everything and so popular that it will include everybody.'

The culture of democracy and the culture of peace will grow stronger from strong local roots. This was Ibsen's message in *Enemy of the People* and Camus's theme in *The Plague*. Profiles in courage are drawn most sharply when we see examples of men and women who confront the fears and prejudices shared by their friends and neighbours and who summon them to live up to higher principles. Local acts of ethical leadership bolster the possibility of a national and international 'politics of principle'.

Against the confusion and hesitations that characterize much of the leadership of our times, certain living examples of taking responsibility for events, with courage and even audacity stand out: Mother Teresa, Mikhail Gorbachev, Dom Helda Camara, President Vaclav Havel of the Czech Republic, South African President Nelson Mandela, former President Frederick De Klerk, and, most recently, Israel's President Yitzhak Rabin and PLO Chairman Yasser Arafat. Each in their own way, and at considerable personal risk, has stepped forward to summon people to dare to give humanism, tolerance, democracy and peace a chance. There are also many local heroes striving in city hall or town meeting to put change for the better on a community agenda. They are points of light, of hope against a general background of stolid, grey routine. But they remain in anonymity. That anonymity, the essence of humanity, ensures the continual advance towards dignity, the dignity of mankind.

Change, therefore, especially the most resistant cultural and attitudinal change, must begin within each one of us as we act locally and think globally. I believe that already it is quietly and persistently under way, particularly among the young, among teachers and among the many community activists around the world in the front line of efforts to overcome widespread political inertia and passivity on the agenda of our era, building democracy, creating a culture of peace, by seeking solutions to problems of population, poverty, ignorance and their consequences – environmental decay, the widening gap between the rich and poor within and between countries and the menace of extremism and its inherent appeal to intolerance and violence.

The beginning of this end-of-20th-century renaissance is a calling into question of received truths and an impatience with inaction. Two economic myths are being subjected to searching criticism because they have been put forward by political leaders as excuses for inaction. One, perhaps the better known, is that the 'free market' is the only solution to the problems of development in the Third World, as well as to the problems of transition to democracy being experienced in Russia and much of the former communist bloc. But is the 'free market' really free? While recent disputes within the GATT (General Agreement on Tariffs and Trade) negotiations have focused on protecting European farmers from their North American competitors, little public attention has been drawn to the protectionism of the entire industrialized world vis-à-vis raw materials and other basic commodities produced in the poorest countries. The terms of trade set by the richest countries, with the biggest markets, virtually condemn the least developed countries and other developing countries to permanent poverty. On the one hand, they are told that they must export these goods in order to earn foreign exchange for debt repayment while, on the other hand, the international terms of trade force the prices down to levels which permit little or no investment, economic, social or human, for the future. Cheap goods for the markets of the rich countries mean that the poor countries must produce more and more to buy less and less advanced equipment and technology.

In addition, the unalloyed 'free market' prescription for Russia, Poland and other former communist bloc countries has led to misery, crime and social instability which threaten nascent democratic institutions. And the expected large injections of outside private capital have not materialized because political and social instability inhibit investor confidence. Meanwhile, public investment in education, scientific research, culture and other crucial underpinnings of democracy has fallen dramatically.

For the nascent democracies of the Third World and those of Central and Eastern Europe, the 'free market' has yet to function as a prop to political, social, cultural and religious freedom. Nor is it reasonable to expect that those who have suffered under different forms of tyranny and totalitarianism will invest their passion for freedom in the market alone. They did not walk through the long, dark tunnel of oppression only to be met by the 'free market' and the shopping mall at the other end! Nor is unbridled capitalism a viable model for the sustainable development of the wealthier societies. The success and stability of their democratic systems have largely depended on their ability to provide a 'social safety net' for the poor and to make the necessary public investment to bring people out of poverty by providing access to education, health care, housing and careers. As John Kenneth Galbraith put it, 'If we really want to have a stable democracy, the only solution is a tax policy allowing the rich to pay for the poor.'

The 'free market', therefore, has been qualified by public policies, democratically voted, which set ethical, humane and legal limits to 'raw capitalism'. Similarly, environmental sustainability will require other forms of market regulation to ensure that economic productivity and human needs are balanced against global warming trends, ozone layer depletion, the Earth's non-renewable resource base and the quality of our soil, oceans and atmosphere.

Perhaps the more important myth is that 'consumer societies' offer a model of culture and society which we would wish proudly to hand on to future generations. Clearly, some choices concerning the usefulness of certain products will have to be made in order to conserve our environment relatively intact for our children. And the myth of happiness through greater and greater consumption of more and more non-necessities has always had its modern critics, however marginal or muted their voices: the Beats, the Hippies and those naturalists such as Scott Nearing and Rachel Carson who, I believe, were the precursors of today's environmentalists. They argued, and I largely agree, that much of the quality of our lives is threatened by an obsession with consuming the latest fad or luxury that comes on the market. It is a race that cannot be won, since each product is soon replaced by a 'new, improved' version and we are drawn towards an ever-receding horizon of promised material well-being. The goal keeps fading as we approach it and we can end up owning almost everything without any notion of the value of anything. Echoing de Tocqueville, Hanna Arendt noted that, if it is clear that freedom can only be attained by those who hide their needs, it is also clear that freedom will never be found by those who are resigned to living according to their needs.

Already a taste for greater austerity and authenticity in the way we live and what we buy has become a force on the market. The demand for organically grown foods has increased enormously, as it has for recyclable, 'environmentally friendly' products. Car manufacturers have vastly increased the efficiency and emission standards of their petrol-driven vehicles. Ethanol- and electric-powered cars have gone into production, showing that a significant demand exists for private transport based on renewable energy sources. This new concern for the impact of what we do, this emerging criticism of received truths, whether economic or political, owe a great deal to the work of scientists and others in demonstrating how interconnected our actions are with worrying trends in our environment. They also owe a great deal to modern telecommunications, which instantly place much that happens in the world within our reach. And they certainly reflect the notion that, with the threats inherent in the cold war receding, we can now turn our attention to an agenda more of our own choosing, reflecting ethical imperatives and reasoned choices that are freed from the constraints of a world divided by hostile and competing ideologies.

We are becoming self-conscious actors in determining our future, rather than mere passengers being driven through time by forces and leaders we cannot question. Indeed, the space for freedom, knowledge and creativity is expanding rapidly, given wider access to higher education, including continuing adult education throughout Europe, North America and many of the urban areas of Asia and Latin America. The trend will accelerate as the personal computer, linked to powerful networks of information and data exchange, moves much of higher learning out of the university and closer to even more settlements, many of which still lack the most basic services, such as electricity.

With the enforced discipline of a war culture being replaced by the freedom and self-discipline of a peace culture, we are all beginning to write a new page in human history. More and more people will have the leisure and the opportunity to devote time to creative, intellectual and artistic activities. Universities, thinkers and artists will speak out loud and clear to others and to those in political leadership roles on the issues, bringing a new intellectual rigour and a new activism to public affairs. The force of reason may well come to replace naked force as the best approach to understanding and resolving conflict.

Themselves open to the scrutiny of a more informed public opinion in an 'information age', international organizations will be called upon to live up to high standards of intellectual rigour and ethical behaviour. Their legitimacy, based as much on their intergovernmental role as on their ability to speak to alert constituencies of specialists and professionals at national and local levels, will depend on their effectiveness in promoting peaceful behaviour among nations based on principles of democracy, justice and fairness. Human resource development, within the context of environmentally sustainable development, will become an essential area for multilateral action.

This possible renaissance at the end of this century is no science fiction. The culture of democracy, as an essential building-block of a culture of peace, must welcome and promote citizen participation in national and *international* affairs. It must construct 'peace in the minds of men' and women by linking the individual to global networks of shared interests and specialities and local communities to the international. And international organizations, like UNESCO, must learn to deal more directly with their professional and citizen constituencies at local levels around the world, to help them form non-governmental communities of concern that can work with governments and regional structures to propose and implement solutions to problems.

A crucial first step, particularly in UNESCO's fields of competence, is to involve the parliaments of the world, particularly the committees specializing in education, science and technology, culture and communications. Parallel to this, modern, inexpensive computer technology could be mobilized to share access to data bases and to interactive networks with the universities and professional communities of the Third World. To spark this renaissance, to harness this multiplicity of promising trends and circumstances to a sustained pattern of change, we must never lose sight of the 'reasons why'. The machinery of citizen involvement at local, national and international levels, however perfected, will mean little if it does not reflect and promote the highest ideals and aspirations of humanity.

Moving from culture to culture, region to region, political system to political system, as my work has required me to do since 1987, has taught me one fundamental truth that lies at the heart of the United Nations Charter and UNESCO's Constitution: the human race is far more united than it is divided by its cultures – its systems of belief – than we have yet fully understood. Perhaps the culture of war and its histories have placed far too much emphasis on what divides us, rather than on the underlying, shared values that can, and should, bring us together. By disarming this kind of history, by beginning to look critically at the baggage of chauvinism and particularism we each carry from a distorted past, we can cut through to the essence of a global community of values. All the world's religions, all of its political ideologies, all of its constitutions propose the same set of aspirations: freedom, dignity and equity. Indeed, communism and capitalism have the same explicit aim of arriving at a world of universal progress towards political liberty and economic well-being. The analyses and the means certainly diverge, as do the reality and imperfections of each system, but the goals are the same. If we are disciplined enough to keep the essential, the priority, in view, then the common values that unite us can become an agenda for the culture of peace.

The obstacle, within ourselves and within our local, national and international communities, will remain the same, and remain daunting: leaning in, rather than leaning out – immuring ourselves in the surface details and routines of the past and closing ourselves off from the diversity and challenges of a wider world. The result has been and can continue to be 'business as usual' in a world which now offers numerous 'windows of opportunity' for change. Should inertia continue to dominate, the renaissance could be delayed and even aborted.

Given that Western Europe and North America have particular responsibilities in the post-cold war world, it is worthwhile to consider the price of passivity from their perspective. The West has so far failed to act swiftly and decisively to promote democracy and peace on its own doorstep. Aid to the former Soviet republics and to the emerging democracies of Eastern Europe has been slow in coming and, in comparison with the Marshall Plan of the late 1940s, surprisingly cautious. Where Secretary of State Marshall could call forth considerable initial sacrifice to meet the threat of communist expansion in Europe, present-day leaders in many Western countries have hesitated to summon their citizens and their industries to a massive investment in future democracy and security.

The lack of a 'rapid-response' capability in confronting the violence in the former Yugoslavia, within Europe itself, has permitted the continuance of 'ethnic cleansing' and civil war which will remain on our conscience for years to come. Nor did the West act in a timely fashion to prevent the Somalian situation from degenerating into mass starvation and political chaos. Again, there was 'business as usual' while inhumanity stalked the Balkans and the horn of Africa. The stakes in these crises, as in the chronic problems of poverty, overpopulation, mass migration and environmental degradation, are very high indeed. The peace and security of the world are at risk, yet the alarm bells remain unheeded. A common vision of priorities, a sense of the essence of community needs and hopes, is lacking among those countries with the economic and political power to move decisively – not only by force! – on all these fronts. The result is unpreparedness and a sense of drift.

The 'new' isolationism is particularly worrying when we consider that all people and all cultures can act together, as never before, to forge a new future for the world. Moreover, this turning inward can continue – as we have seen in the former Yugoslavia, the former Soviet Union and Rwanda – to levels of progressive, often violent, ethnic fragmentation within states. Such an implosion, based as it is on the pseudo-science of race and ethnicity, is particularly troubling to me, not only in my role as Director-General of UNESCO, but as a biochemist, as a Catalan and as a Spaniard. A culture of democracy and peace would not be viable in a situation in which so-called 'ethnic' criteria are used to determine citizenship in a national or a cultural community. Who shall determine the ethnic identity of a 'true' Catalan? And how? Catalonia was for thousands of years a crossroads of ethnic groups and races, religions and languages, sciences and cultures. Each group in that rich exchange has been transformed, culturally and biologically, to the point that being Catalan no longer has any ethnic meaning at all. Rather, it involves the love of the region, its language, its lifestyle, its songs and its dances.

We can celebrate diversity and nurture it at the same time that we affirm the values that are shared between cultures, nations and regions of the world. Coherence and cohesion are impossible without a deep respect for the different ways each culture and religion expresses values common to humanity as a whole. The pursuit of the 'ethnically' pure state is an enterprise that can only revive the prejudices and inhumanity of the all too recent past.

Our security and that of our children require that we tear down the remaining walls that the culture of war taught us were necessary to our survival. Walls, in our minds, our schools, our universities, our religions and our political dogmas, are prisons of perception, blinkers put in place in the false hope that isolation is security and 'ignorance is bliss'. Only through reaching out, through 'leaning out', can we truly build security, peace and democracy. And leaning out means asking difficult questions and accepting our own responsibilities locally and globally. Immigration from the Third World to the developed North or West is an excellent example. While decrying this so-called 'invasion' of those seeking to better themselves, few point out that most of the wealthier countries fall far short of the 0.7 per cent of GDP goal they set themselves for development assistance to the poorer countries. As Mabul ul Haq has written, 'If the opportunities do not fly to the South, the people of the South will fly to where the opportunities are.' And the same stance of looking outward while recognizing our own impact on the 'outside' world would, it is hoped, lead us to understand the roots of fundamentalism in the poor countries. If 'modernization' has failed, if the massive flight from rural areas to the cities of the developing countries has created a population 'at the margins', then how are we to learn to meet that population's needs for dignity, identity and well-being without an opening towards dialogue and mutual respect?

Openness and dialogue are the means, and peace, democracy and security are the goals, for attaining a possible future which reflects the best in our diverse cultures, our different local 'worlds' and our common humanity. We, alone, we, together, can 'lean out' and write the history of the future. The year 2000 is not 'the end of history'. But it should be the end of this story, the story of war. The dawning of peace and all the hopes I have put into writing this book should become reality. As Salvador Espriù says:

> The clarity of the new day suddenly dawns on me,
> a day which will be filled with my happy dream.
> ('Final de Laberint', XXVI)

Index